THE NEW MERMAIDS

The Spanish Tragedy

THE NEW MERMAIDS

General Editors

PHILIP BROCKBANK
Professor of English, University of York

BRIAN MORRIS
Professor of English Literature, University of Sheffield

The Spanish Tragedy

THOMAS KYD

Edited by J. R. MULRYNE

ERNEST BENN LIMITED
LONDON AND TONBRIDGE

First published in this form 1970
by Ernest Benn Limited

25 New Street Square, London, EC4A 3JA &
Sovereign Way, Tonbridge, Kent

Second impression 1974
© *Ernest Benn Limited 1970*
Distributed in Canada by
The General Publishing Company Limited · Toronto
Printed in Great Britain

ISBN *Paperback* 0 - 510 - 33707 - 4

FOR
T. R. HENN
IN GRATITUDE

CONTENTS

Acknowledgements   ix

Abbreviations   xi

Introduction   xiii

   The Author   xiii

   The Play   xv

     Authorship and Date   xv

     Sources and Background   xvii

     Theme and Structure   xix

     Characterisation and Language   xxvi

   The 'Additions'   xxxi

Note on the Text   xxxiii

Further Reading   xxxv

THE SPANISH TRAGEDY   1

   Dramatis Personae   3

   Text   5

ACKNOWLEDGEMENTS

AN EDITOR of *The Spanish Tragedy* owes many debts, especially to earlier editors. I am chiefly indebted to F. S. Boas, whose work forms the basis of modern study of Kyd, and to the indispensable scholarly edition of *The Spanish Tragedy* by Philip Edwards. Professor Edwards put me further in his debt by lending me his photostat copies of the first edition of the play. I am also much indebted to the recent full study of Kyd by Arthur Freeman. Other debts, of an interpretative and scholarly kind, are acknowledged in the footnotes and in the list of further reading. Like all teachers I have learned a great deal from my students, particularly in the second-year class at the University of Edinburgh. I also have to thank the same University for grants-in-aid towards the research behind this book.

J. R. MULRYNE

ABBREVIATIONS

1592	the octavo-in-fours edition of *The Spanish Tragedy* printed in that year.
1594	the octavo-in-fours of that year.
1602	the quarto of that year.
Barish	Jonas A. Barish, '*The Spanish Tragedy*, or 'The Pleasures and Perils of Rhetoric' (see Further Reading).
Boas	*Works of Thomas Kyd*, Oxford, 1901.
Bowers	Fredson T. Bowers, *Elizabethan Revenge Tragedy*, Princeton, 1940.
Cairncross	Andrew S. Cairncross ed., *The First Part of Hieronimo and The Spanish Tragedy* (Regents Renaissance Drama Series), London, 1967.
Clemen	Wolfgang Clemen, *English Tragedy before Shakespeare*, London, 1961.
Edwards	Philip Edwards ed., *The Spanish Tragedy* (The Revels Plays), London, 1959.
Freeman	Arthur Freeman, *Thomas Kyd: Facts and Problems*, Oxford, 1967.
JEGP	*Journal of English and Germanic Philology*.
Johnson	S. F. Johnson, '*The Spanish Tragedy*, or Babylon Revisited' (see Further Reading).
Joseph	Bertram Joseph ed., *The Spanish Tragedy* (The New Mermaids), London, 1964.
McIlwraith	A. K. McIlwraith ed., *Five Elizabethan Tragedies* (The World's Classics), Oxford, 1938.
O.E.D.	*The Oxford English Dictionary*.
PQ	*Philological Quarterly*
Schick	J. Schick ed., *The Spanish Tragedy* (The Temple Dramatists), London, 1898.
s.d.	stage direction.
s.p.	speech prefix.
SP	*Studies in Philology*.
Tilley	M. P. Tilley, *A Dictionary of the Proverbs in England in the Sixteenth and Seventeenth Centuries*, Ann Arbor, 1950.

INTRODUCTION

THE AUTHOR

THOMAS KYD belongs to the first generation of Elizabethan play-wrights. He was born in 1558, some six years before Shakespeare and Marlowe, fifteen years before Jonson, and more than twenty years before Middleton and Webster. His death in 1594, at the age of thirty-six, preceded the staging of almost all the Elizabethan master-pieces, save his own *Spanish Tragedy* and the plays of Marlowe. Kyd's importance in the theatre lies as much in his position as innovator and pioneer as in his actual achievement.

Kyd was baptised at the Church of St Mary Woolnoth in London on 6 November 1558, the child of a comfortably middle-class family.[1] His father, Francis Kyd, achieved some distinction as a scrivener, serving as Warden of the Company of Scriveners in 1580, a member of an affluent but often disliked profession, with duties in the field of copying documents, and with some importance therefore in the complicated world of Elizabethan legal affairs. As a well-educated man, Francis sought a good education for his son, sending Thomas in 1565 at the age of seven to Merchant Taylors' School, a new foundation under the care of Richard Mulcaster, the noted educationalist, whose pupils at this time included Edmund Spenser, Lancelot Andrewes and Thomas Lodge. Here, it seems probable, Kyd will have become familiar with Latin, French and Italian, and may have had some Greek; Merchant Taylors' may also have first introduced him to the stage, for plays formed part of the boys' activities, some of them being acted before Queen Elizabeth at Court.

We know virtually nothing of Kyd's early manhood, and can only speculate that he followed his father's profession of scrivener—his handwriting in the few scraps that remain is markedly neat and formal. Certainly he seems not to have attended either university. By 1585, at the age of twenty-seven, he was writing plays for the Queen's Company, the leading London players, though none of his work for this company is known to survive. During 1587-8 he entered the service of a lord, variously identified as Henry, fourth

---

[1] For full documentation of the known facts about Kyd see Arthur Freeman, *Thomas Kyd: Facts and Problems,* Oxford, 1967.

earl of Sussex, or Ferdinando Stanley, Lord Strange, either of whom he may have served as secretary or tutor. His patron acted, we know, as patron also to a company of players.[2]

Information about Kyd's later life comes almost entirely from writings connected with a single incident: his detention and probable torture at the hands of the Privy Council. Details of the affair are in parts uncertain, but it appears that Kyd was arrested during an investigation ordered by the Privy Council on 11 May 1593, to discover the source of certain 'libels'—writings, probably, directed against foreigners resident in London. Among Kyd's papers the officers came upon what were described as 'vile hereticall Conceiptes denyinge the deity of Jhesus Christe o[r] Savio[r]', and on suspicion of having written such grave blasphemy Kyd was imprisoned.[3] Kyd apparently claimed that the writings were not his but Marlowe's. After Marlowe's death on 30 May 1593, he wrote to Sir John Puckering, the effectual head of the Privy Council, seeking release from prison and explaining how Marlowe's papers came to be in his possession—the two authors were 'wrytinge in one chamber twoe yeares synce'. He added that Marlowe's known sentiments dovetailed perfectly with those of the 'hereticall Conceiptes'. Both in this letter and in another Kyd amplified his charge; Marlowe is accused, with vivid if sometimes forced illustration, of being blasphemous, disorderly, of treasonous opinions, an irreligious reprobate, 'intemp[er]ate & of a cruel hart'. The morality of the affair has been much disputed, some writers thinking that Kyd acted disgracefully. Kyd may, however, have suspected that Marlowe informed on him, he may have guessed or known that Marlowe was a spy for Walsingham (and therefore deserved what accusations came his way), or he may in his anxiety to escape prison and torture have slandered his erstwhile acquaintance only when he knew him to be dead and thus beyond suffering as a result of anything he said.[4] It is doubtful whether the truth of the matter will ever be known. In any case Kyd was himself dead little more than a year later, his death hastened, it

[2] Freeman argues for the earl of Sussex; Philip Edwards (Revels edition, London, 1959, p. xx) says the patron was 'possibly' Lord Strange, citing Tucker Brooke and Boas.

[3] He may also have had in his possession some of the 'libels' originally sought. Quotations in this paragraph are from contemporary documents reproduced in Freeman, pp. 26–30. W. D. Briggs (*SP*, XX (1920), 153–9) has shown the writings are transcripts from an early sixteenth-century theistic treatise, already in print, and scarcely 'atheistic'.

[4] Marlowe was in fact arrested (18 May) shortly after Kyd, whether on Kyd's information is not known. He was released on 20 May, ten days only before he was stabbed to death at Deptford.

seems probable, by his experiences in prison. He was buried at St Mary Colchurch in London on 15 August 1594.

Kyd's writings may well have been much more extensive than those that have come down to us as his. Besides *The Spanish Tragedy* we have on good authority only a translation of Tasso's *Padre di Famiglia* (published in 1588 under the title *The Householder's Philosophy*). Kyd may have written *Soliman and Perseda*, a play that shares its main source with Hieronimo's last-act play-within-the-play in *The Spanish Tragedy*; the evidence is not, however, conclusive. A play known as *I Hieronimo* may, in one form or another, be Kyd's; a kind of fore-piece to *The Spanish Tragedy*, it was perhaps written to capitalise on the success of the greater play. The text we have, published in 1605 by Thomas Pavier, is written in a style rather unlike Kyd's, and may represent a revision of the play by another hand.[5] Notoriously, Kyd may also be the author of an early version of *Hamlet*, a version now irretrievably lost. Although the evidence rests, in the first instance, on widely-disputed allusions in Thomas Nashe's preface for Robert Greene's *Menaphon*, the balance of probabilities seems to incline towards Kyd's having in fact written such a play. Altogether, the skill deployed in *The Spanish Tragedy*, taken together with early references to Kyd as a dramatist of some importance, strongly suggests that much more of his work than we now know found its way on to the stage.

THE PLAY

Authorship and Date

Until 1773 no editor or dramatic historian attached the name of Thomas Kyd to his one independent and now undisputed play. Early printings carried no author's name. Thomas Heywood, in his *Apology for Actors* (1612), did, however, refer to 'M. Kid, in his Spanish Tragedy', and this attribution was taken up in Thomas Hawkins's *The Origin of the English Drama* (Oxford, 1773). There is now no reason to doubt Hawkins's ascription.

The date of *The Spanish Tragedy* has long been a matter of dispute and conjecture. The point is significant to literary historians for on an accurate dating of this play depends much in their account of the development of English tragedy. Arthur Freeman writes:

[5] Andrew S. Cairncross, the play's latest editor (Regents Renaissance Drama Series, London, 1967) thinks Pavier's text a 'memorial reconstruction' of a play by Kyd. His evidence is unconvincing.

If the play precedes *The Jew of Malta* and *The Massacre at Paris* it contains the first Machiavellian villain; if it precedes *John a Kent and John a Cumber* it contains the earliest modern play-within-play; and if it precedes *Titus Andronicus* it may also be styled the first modern revenge tragedy. Given a date before 1587 and *Tamburlaine*, one might incontro- vertibly call Kyd's play the first extant modern tragedy, without qualification.[6]

But despite the attractions of a firm date no scholar has so far succeeded in establishing one. Certainly the play must have been written before 23 February 1592, for on that day it was performed by Lord Strange's men for Henslowe. It was probably written after 1582, as it adapts material from Thomas Watson's *Hekatompathia*, entered in the Stationers' Register during that year.[7] But between these extreme dates all is inference.[8] T. W. Baldwin places the date as early as 1583-4, while Philip Edwards, John Dover Wilson and W. W. Greg all prefer a date at the other end of the scale in 1590 or '91. Boas suggests 1585-7, and Freeman finds his suggestion plausible. None of their arguments is irrefutable; reasoned con- jectures and tentative conclusions only are possible. Freeman, for example, finds the tone of the Spanish allusions a 'pre-Armada tone' (because it is 'a trifle shrill' rather than, as it would have been after the victory, confident or even patronising); yet he admits this gives him only 'a modest excuse for dating the play before 1588'. Philip Edwards, referring to suggested parallels with *2 Tamburlaine*, *The Jew of Malta*, *King John*, *3 Henry VI* and Thomas Watson's *Meliboeus*, concludes: 'No reader will need to be warned of the entire absence of proof in these parallels; they are brought forward none the less, straws as they are, because the date they would hint at, namely 1590, seems to me not at all inappropriate to the style and manner of *The Spanish Tragedy*.'[9] In the absence of firmer evidence we can only place the date somewhere between the outer limits of 1582 and '92, with a balance of conjecture in favour of the later

[6] Freeman, op. cit., pp. 70-1.

[7] Even this is uncertain: Kyd, an acquaintance of Watson's, might have read his work in manuscript.

[8] The fullest discussions of dating come in Edwards, op. cit., pp. xxi-xxvii and in Freeman, op. cit., pp. 70-9; see also F. S. Boas, *The Works of Thomas Kyd*, Oxford, 1901, pp. xxviii-xxxi; T. W. Baldwin, 'On the Chronology of Thomas Kyd's Plays', *MLN*, XL (1925), 343-9; W. W. Greg, 'The Works of Thomas Kyd', *MLQ*, IV (1901), 186-90. J. D. Wilson offers his dating in his edition of *King John*, pp. liii and 115-16.

[9] Edwards, op. cit., p. xxvii. Harold Brooks approves a late dating; see 'Marlowe and Early Shakespeare' in *Christopher Marlowe*, ed. Brian Morris, London, 1968, p. 79.

years; the historical importance of Kyd's play, while obviously considerable, must remain in detail unproven.

Sources and Background

The Spanish Tragedy is unusual among Elizabethan plays in that
scholars have been unable to discover a source for the play's action.
It is true that an analogous story may be found in Henry Wotton's
translation of the tales of Jacques Yver, published in 1578 as *A
Courtlie Controversie of Cupid's Cautels*; but even if Kyd used Yver,
or some work based on Yver, it seems probable that his adaptation is
distinguished more by its originality than by its indebtedness.[10] On a
smaller scale Kyd has, it seems plain, used Yver's stories, perhaps at
one remove;[11] one of the tales provides the basis for the play of
Soliman and Perseda that Hieronimo stages in Act IV. Here again,
however, Kyd's originality is evident: he widely altered the story's
conclusion to fit the demands of his own play. Kyd's remarkable
skill in devising the intricate structure of his play may arise in part
from his not being hampered by the demands of an existing story.

A more pervasive influence on *The Spanish Tragedy*, if not in the
strict sense a source, is the work of the Roman dramatist Seneca.
Certain dramatic devices of importance to Kyd's play come either
direct from Seneca's works or from Senecan imitators like the
Italian playwright Giraldi Cinthio (1504–73). The Ghost of
Andrea, for example, and the Ghost's prologue, have counterparts in
Seneca, even though Kyd's use of them is not strictly Senecan. More
important, the whole theme of revenge, the prime mover of Kyd's
play, is a Senecan theme, though here again Kyd alters the earlier
dramatist's practice—he is less interested than Seneca in the curse
that pursues a family through several generations. Kyd also shares
with Seneca a certain interest in bloodshed and various kinds of
horror; though *The Spanish Tragedy* is quite free of exaggerated
relish of such matters. Moreover, Kyd quotes Seneca directly, makes
use of Senecan tags in translation, and owes a general stylistic debt
to Senecan rhetoric: his use of stichomythia (answering single lines
of verse-dialogue) is, for example, a Senecan technique.[12] Here

[10] For a summary of the story in question, concerning a young prince
Adilon and his beloved Clarinda, daughter of Francisco Gonzaga, see
Freeman, op. cit., p. 51.
[11] Edwards, op. cit., p. xlviii, thinks Kyd may have used the anonymous
Soliman and Perseda (frequently attributed to Kyd himself) which in turn
uses Yver in Wotton's translation.
[12] Discussions of Kyd and the Senecan tradition will be found in T. S. Eliot,
'Seneca in Elizabethan Translation' in *Selected Essays*, London, 1932,

again, however, Kyd is remarkable not so much for what he owed to Seneca as for what he made of his debt. Where Seneca's plays are largely verbal, Kyd's work is decisively of the theatre; 'behind the drama of words', to borrow Eliot's phrase, 'is the drama of action'. Elizabethan dramatists stand considerably indebted to those writers who between 1559 and 1581 translated Seneca into English: the whole technique of playwriting, it could be claimed, was revolutionised. But within the shell of Senecan practice the Elizabethans, Kyd among the first of them, built a wholly new and far more robust drama.

One isolated incident for which a convincing source may be found is Lorenzo's cunning disposal of Pedringano. A rather similar story is told in the banned *A Copie of a Letter* (1584) concerning the earl of Leicester and one Gates, a thief in his employ. Like Lorenzo, Leicester arranged his accomplice's death while pretending to stand his protector. In developing the character of Lorenzo out of this source Kyd shows his keen feeling for the interests of his day: Lorenzo is the first (or almost the first) of a long line of stage-Machiavels in the Elizabethan drama.

One other contemporary interest needs brief comment, as it undoubtedly influenced Kyd in writing his play, and must be taken into account when reading it. Fredson Bowers has shown beyond quibble the continuing sympathy for private revenge in Elizabethan England.[13] In the recent lawless past the only means to achieving justice (or retaliation rather) for a crime against the person had been through private revenge; and even though the law now quite specifically forbade such vengeance (as it had not always done), and though moralists and preachers drew attention to the seemingly unambiguous Biblical prohibition ('Vengeance is mine, I will repay, saith the Lord'), a strong emotional prejudice in favour of the private revenger still persisted in Elizabethan sentiment. Writers quite openly argued that when the law was unable or reluctant to settle injuries (because, perhaps, of a lack of formal evidence) an individual might justifiably take over the law's functions; even Francis Bacon, strong for the rights of law, admits that 'the most tolerable sort of revenge is for those wrongs which there is no law to punish; else a man's enemy is still before hand, and it is two for one.'[14] On such

pp. 65–108; F. T. Bowers, op. cit., pp. 41–7; F. L. Lucas, *Seneca and Elizabethan Tragedy*, Cambridge, 1922; P. Simpson, 'The Theme of Revenge in Elizabethan Tragedy' in *Studies in Elizabethan Drama*, Oxford, 1955; and in Edwards and Freeman. For direct Senecan reference in the text see notes to this edition at III, xiii, 6, 12–13, 35.
[13] *Elizabethan Revenge Tragedy*, Princeton, 1940, esp. pp. 3–40.
[14] Quoted Bowers, p. 36.

ambiguous or at least unresolved attitudes as this Kyd has drawn in permitting his chief sympathetic characters to seek private revenge. He has also been especially careful in making Hieronimo the kind of man who would escape censure in this climate of opinion: not only is he grievously wronged, but he does all in his power to effect revenge through the legal system of which he is himself an honourable representative. Once only does Hieronimo have brief misgivings (at the beginning of III, xiii) and on that occasion misgiving has to bow to practical necessity.[15] With Andrea the matter is less clear-cut, as it is with Bel-imperia; here Kyd is relying even more heavily on that almost pagan pleasure in getting even which the Elizabethans indulged under the guise of revenge.

Finally, the evidence is inconclusive on the question of whether Kyd draws on recent unrest between Spain and Portugal for the general historical background of the play. Freeman believes there are references to the campaign which included the Battle of Alcantara (24 August 1580) and to the naval battle at Terceira in the Azores (July–August 1582). Philip Edwards questions such allusions, and draws attention to the absence from *The Spanish Tragedy* of references to Spanish perfidiousness and papist irreligion, such as one would expect in an Elizabethan play wishing to call attention to recent Spanish history. Edwards thinks the setting 'unhistorical'; for the purposes of his play Kyd needed a war-situation and sketched one involving Spain and Portugal without much thought for recent political events. Certainly there seems little overt attempt to be especially informative or controversial about Spanish history.[16]

Theme and Structure

In the scene that closes the third Act of *The Spanish Tragedy* the Ghost of Andrea upbraids Revenge for neglecting his office. Revenge's answer might serve as gloss on the whole play:

> Thus worldlings ground, what they have dreamed, upon.
> Content thyself, Andrea: though I sleep,
> Yet is my mood soliciting their souls; . . .
> Behold, Andrea, for an instance how
> Revenge hath slept, and then imagine thou
> What 'tis to be subject to destiny.   (III, xv, 18–20, 26–28)

All in the play's main action ground their thoughts and deeds on

---

[15] Bowers thinks we lose sympathy with Hieronimo when he begins to employ craft to effect his revenge; this opinion no longer finds much support among critics.

[16] See Freeman, op. cit., pp. 51–4, and Edwards, op. cit., pp. xxiv–xxv.

'dreams'; most are solicited by Revenge's mood; all are subject to destiny. Within the ironic co-ordinates defined by these terms the play's meaning takes shape.

The Spanish Tragedy stands among the first of a group of Elizabethan plays now known as tragedies of Revenge. In an obvious way, the play's action is set in motion and sustained by revenge-intrigues: Andrea seeks revenge for his death in battle at the hands of Balthazar; Bel-imperia looks for vengeance for Andrea's, her lover's, death; Balthazar and Lorenzo seek revenge on Horatio for winning Bel-imperia's love; Hieronimo pursues vengeance for the murder, by Lorenzo and Balthazar, of his son Horatio. From these intrigues develops all the rest of the play's narrative; as Philip Edwards writes, '*The Spanish Tragedy* is a play about the passion for retribution, and vengeance shapes the entire action.'[17] But quite as remarkable as this dominance of plot is the range of attitudes that prompt the characters to vengeance: the slight to Andrea's honour, and the ending of his love-plans, that come with death in battle; the aversion Bel-imperia feels for her lover's deathsman; the envy Balthazar cherishes for a successful rival in love and war; the outrage felt by Hieronimo on the assassination of his innocent son. Each of these characters is in some sense injured by one or more of the others, and each seeks to amend the injury. Revenge is central to *The Spanish Tragedy*, as to others among the great Elizabethan plays, because it offers a convenient way of dramatising human conflict and competitiveness; blood-revenge merely exaggerates, makes more dramatic, familiar antagonisms. Criticism of Kyd's play has sometimes complained that it is structurally weak and morally unallowable because its initiating and concluding actions centre on an incident which ought not to be revenged. Andrea was killed, it has been pointed out, in formal if uneven battle.[18] The tragedy gets under way, it is said, only when the murder of Horatio provides a more allowable cause for revenge. Such criticism is misguided because Kyd's interest lies in the consequences, proportionate or not, of human enmity. When the play concludes in the satisfaction of Andrea and Revenge, we may well feel that morally there is a good deal to excuse or deplore: the waste and deaths that minister to that satisfaction. We shall feel equally the bitter consistency of motive and action that has led to this point. Kyd has dramatised, through the revenge idiom, one full and tragic episode in the satisfaction of human pride.

Seeing the play in this light explains the pertinence of the Vergilian framework within which Kyd has placed the main action. Andrea's

17 Edwards, op. cit., p. li.
18 See I, iv, 21–6 and note.

search for a resting-place in the classical underworld stands for the
disappointed man's thirst for satisfaction. Thwarted by death of
fulfilment as lover or 'martialist', he is unable to find rest in the
underworld. Only when the goddess Proserpine bids Revenge to
sponsor his privileged view of subsequent events can he achieve
rest. The gods in the play are gods that watch over, and promote or
thwart, human desires—or dreams. Only by circumstance do they
become gods of morality (when we think the desires and their
realisation justified); even more rarely do they come within an
acceptable Christian sense of the word God. Almost all the play's
major characters appeal at one time or other to Aeacus, Minos,
Rhadamanth, Pluto or Proserpine; when they do so they are suppli-
cating the amoral overseers of Fortune. Heaven in this tragedy is
normally the province of such gods as these; fittingly in a play that
concerns itself with the working-out of Revenge.

Interpretation of *The Spanish Tragedy* as a revenge play success-
fully identifies the mainspring of the play's action. It fails, however,
on the surface at least, to account for certain of the play's scenes,
especially those that take place in Portugal. 'The Portuguese court',
writes Philip Edwards, 'could have been introduced more economic-
ally and the relevance of theme is very slight.'[19] Recent studies by
Ejner Jensen and G. K. Hunter have tried to demonstrate the
pertinence of these and other scenes by displacing the play's focus
from revenge to justice. The tragedy's 'chief unifying theme',
according to Jensen, 'is not revenge but the problem of justice';
Hunter agrees that 'the play is not centrally concerned with the
enactment of revenge. Much more obsessive is the question of
justice.'[20] Justice, or judgment, serves indeed as a major preoccupation. Not only is Hieronimo himself a judge but instances of judging
and misjudging occur repeatedly. Andrea seeks judgment from
Aeacus, Rhadamanth and Minos, and, on their reaching deadlock,
from the higher court of Pluto and Proserpine. The King of Spain is
called on to arbitrate the rival claims to Balthazar of Lorenzo and
Horatio. The Viceroy of Portugal is led into, and then narrowly
avoids, a miscarriage of justice in the case of Alexandro and Villuppo.
Hieronimo questions the 'justice' of the Heavens, while himself
administering justice in others' causes. Pedringano is hanged despite
promises to subvert the course of justice. Hieronimo's playlet of
Soliman and Perseda may be construed as a kind of last judgment, its
sentences interpreted by Andrea and confirmed, we expect, by

[19] Edwards, op. cit., p. liii.
[20] Jensen, 'Kyd's *Spanish Tragedy*: The Play Explains Itself', *JEGP*, LXIV
(1965), 8; Hunter, 'Ironies of Justice in *The Spanish Tragedy*', *Renaissance
Drama*, VIII (1965), 92.

Proserpine. Justice, then, or rather the securing of justice, might be named the play's central interest. But justice and revenge are not really separate issues. In the judgment Andrea seeks they are identical; Revenge sponsors the decisions of Proserpine's court. For Hieronimo the only problem is the straightforward practical one of arranging circumstances so that justice brings about revenge. In other cases, justice, though in danger of mistake, is the simple instrument of vengeance: the Viceroy condemns Alexandro for, as he thinks, the murder of his son; Pedringano is condemned and executed for the killing of Serberine. When Lorenzo and Balthazar die, Hieronimo's vengeance serves in place of the justice they have till then averted. Sometimes, as in the King's arbitration or in Hieronimo's promises to the suitors, justice is a matter of 'fair play', a situation that falls between justice as retribution and justice in the emotionally-loaded sense that Andrea, Bel-imperia and sometimes Hieronimo mean the word. For to say that revenge and justice are not separate issues is not to say that they are always identical. Justice in the familiar sense can scarcely be said to be done in the killing of Castile at the play's end (even though he was Andrea's enemy) nor in the deaths of Hieronimo nor Bel-imperia nor Horatio, all of them sanctioned by Revenge. Justice satisfies us in a play because it reflects a situation we desire in our everyday lives: order upheld by the correction of socially-unacceptable behaviour. Revenge is a more individual matter, a matter more of emotional satisfaction, to which justice may contribute, but which may not always involve, may even contradict, the interests of law and of society. When Hieronimo protests the seeming absence of Heavenly justice, he is protesting certainly the failure of human courts to bring to justice his son's murderers. But he is really talking about a far larger issue, and one that becomes a leading preoccupation of dramatists like Shakespeare and Webster:

> Yet still tormented is my tortured soul
> With broken sighs and restless passions,
> That winged mount, and hovering in the air,
> Beat at the windows of the brightest heavens,
> Soliciting for justice and revenge;
> But they are placed in those empyreal heights,
> Where, counter-mured with walls of diamond,
> I find the place impregnable; and they
> Resist my woes, and give my words no way.

(III, vii, 10–18)

The bafflement of the individual before the ways of Heaven (or Fortune) becomes more embittered in plays later than this. Here the justice Hieronimo seeks is one that operates (as line 14 suggests) through revenge, and the whole play ministers to their eventual triumph. In *The Spanish Tragedy* justice and revenge interact, support, and contradict one another in an intricate mirroring of human conflict. In the end, Heaven, it appears, is not deaf, though the Heaven that listens, it is true, can hardly in human terms be called just.

Kyd's play is held together by instances of judging that finally contribute to the success of revenge; or, in the case of the Portuguese scenes and those that deal with Pedringano, that shadow revenge's ultimate triumph. But judging is by no means always done in full knowledge of the facts. On the contrary, *The Spanish Tragedy* is remarkable for the extent to which Kyd exploits the ignorance of the characters for ironic effect.[21] By virtue of the framing action in particular we in the audience enjoy knowledge hidden from participants in the main play. We know that the play's outcome will be disastrous for anyone who opposes Andrea's revenge, even though the path to vengeance may be tortuous and revenge delayed. Andrea's doubts and Revenge's reassurance (in the scenes that close Acts I, II and III), as well as their continued presence as spectators, merely dramatise overtly the relationship the audience adopts to the events on stage. We are held between concern and detachment as the plot moves forward: concerned, like Andrea, that Horatio is killed, Bel-imperia sequestered, and Hieronimo thwarted, but detached like Revenge because we know that Andrea's cause, under his sponsorship, must eventually win through. The effect of this is to place us in an ironic relationship with almost everything that happens: all action takes place within a determined framework to which we, but not the actors, hold the key. We feel in I, i, for instance, the threat of oncoming disaster behind the boastful self-confidence and military display of the Spanish court, even if we cannot exactly predict the catastrophe that at the play's end destroys the whole Spanish succession. When the Spanish King overweeningly exclaims

> Then blest be heaven, and guider of the heavens,
> From whose fair influence such justice flows.
>
> (I, ii, 10–11)

we recognise that heavenly justice may not be as simple nor, for him, as comprehensible as he thinks: the battle he gives such easy thanks for is the battle of Andrea's death. Equally, we sense behind every movement Balthazar makes, or Lorenzo or Bel-imperia or Hieronimo, the long shadow of Andrea's revenge, sometimes aiding,

---

[21] See G. K. Hunter, op. cit., for a penetrating analysis of this aspect of the play.

sometimes threatening. But besides such general ironies as these
Kyd cultivates more particular and overt ironic moments. As
Horatio courts Bel-imperia in II, ii, for instance, we know that
Pedringano has already betrayed their love; while the two lovers
confess their affection and anticipate love's pleasures the hidden
Balthazar and Lorenzo contradict all they say: the intricate structure
of statement and counterstatement provides a grim version of the
overhearing scenes of intrigue comedy. When in a later scene (II, iv)
they invoke night and darkness to countenance their love-making we
scarcely need the sombre if crude irony of Horatio's

> O stay awhile and I will die with thee

to underline the equivocal sense in which we have been observing
the whole episode. Ironies can run in a contrary direction also, most
complexly perhaps in the Portuguese scenes (I, iii and III, i). There
we see the Viceroy mourning, while we know his son is in fact alive;
and yet the mourning is pertinent too for we know the son's life is
threatened ineluctably by Andrea. When the mourning turns to joy
in a later scene we appreciate that under the superficial cause of joy
lie causes of dread: for by now the Viceroy's son has committed the
murder of another son, Horatio, a crime which must inevitably lead
to his own destruction. Ironies multiply elsewhere; we are always
conscious of the ignorance, sometimes greater, sometimes less, of the
characters. Each of them attempts to clear a little space for himself,
to impose his will a little, without being able to escape the pattern of
consequence established by Revenge. Even the intriguers, the
Machiavels, like Lorenzo and his shadow Villuppo, are only attempting, in their own bad way, to control the movements of Fortune.
Villuppo is cheated by the merest coincidence: the Ambassador
returns from Spain moments before Alexandro is to be executed;
Lorenzo's schemes, at first successful, are ultimately defeated by
Hieronimo's persistence and Bel-imperia's, and by the operations of
chance. Hieronimo is himself another intriguer, a wily revenger
forced by circumstances to adopt unlawful tactics; an intriguer
favoured, however, by the prevailing Fate, as Bel-imperia's letter
and then Pedringano's lead him to apt and successful action. Kyd
provides us with an almost emblematic, near-burlesque, statement
of the whole situation: Pedringano jesting with death (or Fate) as the
boy points to the box—empty, despite Pedringano's confidence that
it contains his pardon. Each of the play's characters is as vulnerable
to an engrossing Fate as Pedringano; and almost all are as blithely
unaware as he that they lack the power to turn that Fate aside,
whether their purposes are good or ill. The experience of watching
The Spanish Tragedy is the ironic one of seeing 'truth' gradually

vindicated over the ignorance or devising of the characters, whether it is vindicated in the matter of Villuppo, or the death of Serberine, or the main-plot killing of Horatio. 'Truth' is, of course, as we have seen, a concept that in this play serves the interests of Revenge.

To present his theme Kyd has structured the play masterfully. Not only are the ironies brilliantly cultivated, but episodes are contrived with striking skill to reflect and balance each other. The Viceroy's mourning for his son anticipates and extends Hieronimo's mourning; both weep the death of a son and blame Fortune's injuries: the subtleties of the Elizabethan sub-plot are predicted. Andrea's revenge, the Viceroy's revenge on Alexandro or Villuppo, Lorenzo's witty disposal of Pedringano, Hieronimo's revenge for his son— these serve like angled mirrors to reiterate but never exactly repeat similar concerns and situations. Alexandro, the Viceroy, Isabella, Bel-imperia, Hieronimo, Pedringano all see themselves at one time or another the victim of an oppressive Fortune, and each in his different way tries to rationalise his position; the author's devising hand has so contrived the action that we discover a whole range of linked but dissimilar attitudes. To keep the plot firm, Kyd has arranged that Horatio becomes quite explicitly a second Andrea (I, iv, 58ff.); he may even (the evidence is not quite conclusive) make use of a convenient hand-prop to connect the two revenges visually: the scarf Bel-imperia gave Andrea to wear in battle was taken from his dead body by Horatio and confirmed by Bel-imperia for her new lover's wearing; it may be the same 'bloody handkercher' that Hieronimo takes from his dead son's body and keeps to the end as revenge-token. A contrivance equally deft operates within scenes and episodes: Wolfgang Clemen has shown how scene after scene observes carefully-planned, almost geometrical, patterning, a structural cunning that reflects on the level of plot the rhetorical niceties of the characters' language.[22] Act two, scene one, for instance, is structured on the 'corner-posts' of Balthazar's twin speeches, at beginning and end, about Bel-imperia and Horatio; 'thus the two goals of Balthazar's future endeavours are brought into sharp relief, not only in dialogue enlivened by action, but also through the rhetorical emphasis of the set speeches'.[23] So too Kyd has shown he knows how to use stage-action to underline the symmetries of the plot: Balthazar first enters with Lorenzo and Horatio on either side, each laying claim to being his captor, and thus predicting the dissensions the whole play is about to elaborate. Even the two plays-within-the-play reflect and echo each other: the first, though

[22] Wolfgang Clemen, *English Tragedy before Shakespeare* (London, 1961), esp. pp. 100–12 and 267–77.
[23] Clemen, op. cit., p. 102.

counselling humility, written in honour of Spain's military glory, the second contriving the destruction of the royal house. And this second play itself provides one of the best examples of Kyd's structural cunning, as it reflects and interprets the tragedy's central theme. There is a certain, though not exact, appropriateness in Bel-imperia playing Perseda, Balthazar playing Soliman and Hieronimo playing the 'Bashaw': they enact in these parts roles that parallel their actions in the main play.[24] More telling is the episode's general bearing. There has been disagreement about whether the 'sundry languages' of the polyglot play were ever spoken on stage; disagreement is scarcely possible over the almost surrealist fashion in which the action of the play—death stealing in unperceived amidst a Babel-like confusion of tongues—repeats the major idiom of the whole tragedy.[25] By this point Hieronimo has become virtually Fate's representative dealing to ignorant victims the consequences of Revenge. The manner in which this playlet, three fictional levels distant from a theatre-audience, crystallises Kyd's ironic intentions indicates why Kyd became so fruitful an influence on later dramatic craftsmen.

Characterisation and Language

The perils of a tragedy conceived as *The Spanish Tragedy* is conceived are that the audience may become *mere* spectators, the plot-structure *merely* contrived and the ironies *merely* patronising. The figure of Hieronimo ensures that such dangers are slipped. Hieronimo is the play's centre because he tries more persistently and with more emotion than anyone else, within the limits imposed by this play, to find truth and establish equity—though of a crude kind. In so doing he draws an audience's sympathy and involvement, despite arguments, now largely discounted by critics, that he forfeits our respect when he begins to act unlawfully.[26] Hieronimo engages our interest as the beleaguered man who tries in all honesty, and with outstanding pertinacity, to set right the wrongs of his time. In this he of course anticipates Hamlet, the character with whom he has notoriously been linked by dramatic historians. It is true that for

---

[24] Too exact comparison would show Lorenzo miscast as Erasto; Middleton makes a more thorough job of such parallels in a similar situation in the last Act of *Women Beware Women*.

[25] For an elaborate discussion of this point see S. F. Johnson, '*The Spanish Tragedy*, or Babylon Revisited', in *Essays on Shakespeare and Elizabethan Drama*, ed. Richard Hosley, London, 1963, pp. 23–36.

[26] For the argument on this point see John D. Ratliff, 'Hieronimo Explains Himself', *SP* 54 (1957), 112–18.

Hieronimo the world is not as question-fraught as it is for Shakespeare's hero, largely because Kyd scarcely allows Hieronimo to
question his own nature and motives, nor is he skilled enough to
make the environment within which Hieronimo acts anything like
so disturbingly equivocal as the world of *Hamlet*. Yet the seeds of
self-questioning are there (the soliloquy in III, xii, for example,
anticipates Hamlet's musings on suicide), and so are the first signs
of a difficult if not quite equivocal world: the intrigues of Lorenzo,
the hints of a double standard for judging strong and weak, the
business-preoccupied mentality that thwarts justice and revenge in
the latter part of III, xii. If Hieronimo is nothing so complex and
fascinating a character as Hamlet, he does share many of the same
challenges, and he does pursue his similar quest with comparable
unwillingness to prevaricate or compromise, except on the surface.
And unlike Hamlet he raises an issue very fruitful for tragedies
written later in the Elizabethan decades: his anguished sense that
Heaven itself is deaf:

> Where shall I run to breathe abroad my woes,
> My woes whose weight hath wearied the earth?
> Or mine exclaims, that have surcharged the air
> With ceaseless plaints for my deceased son? . . .
>
> (III, vii, 1ff.)

Hieronimo's quest soon slips off into less demanding matters of
tactics and practicality, but here at least—the whole speech should
be studied—Kyd succeeds in writing a poetry of the theatre that
adequately conveys Hieronimo's sense of a world wholly occupied
by his new-found sorrow, a sorrow made more intense because at this
stage he can summon no comforting belief that a supernatural order
oversees his experience or will in any way alleviate his pain. It is true
that even a sympathetic critic must find moments in this speech of
over-emphasis and cliché; and what is true here is true *a fortiori* of
other among Hieronimo's soliloquies. A modern reader finds it
difficult to adjust to the larger-than-life emphasis, as well as the
self-conscious artificiality of structure, in Kyd's stage-rhetoric.
Exaggeratedly deep emotion wedded to exceptional artifice of
structure appears to us contradiction and even insincerity; we react
all too gratefully to those parodies of Hieronimo's speeches that
Elizabethan authors soon began to invent. Yet we miss the point of
Kyd's dramatic skill if we do not see how subtly he has calculated, in
the quoted speech, the alliterative patterns: not so emphatic as to
call undue attention to themselves, but strong enough to afford the
actor some purchase for moulding the speech-pattern; or if we do
not see how naturally, and yet with seeming inevitability, he has

ordered the tempo of the speech: noting particularly the way in
which urgent exclamation is reined in at the natural pauses of lines
9, 14 and 18. Kyd's strengths as a writer of dramatic verse are at
their most remarkable in this and other soliloquies put into
Hieronimo's mouth. Even the notorious 'O eyes, no eyes' soliloquy
(III, ii, 1–52), the most formally patterned and among the most
emotional of all Hieronimo's speeches, need not prove impossibly
difficult on the modern stage;[27] Kyd's instinct for dramatic speech
ensures that here too the cadences of his rhetoric are such as can be
turned to account: the rise and fall of emotional intensity, and the
implied tempo of individual sentences, never forget stage-require-
ments; they provide opportunities rather for the actor's virtuosity.
And Kyd can be affectingly simple where simplicity seems in place:

> Ay, now I know thee, now thou nam'st thy son;
> Thou art the lively image of my grief:
> Within thy face my sorrows I may see.
> Thy eyes are gummed with tears, thy cheeks are wan,
> Thy forehead troubled, and thy muttering lips
> Murmur sad words abruptly broken off
> By force of windy sighs thy spirit breathes;
> And all this sorrow riseth for thy son:
> And selfsame sorrow feel I for my son.   (III, xiii, 161–9)

Bazulto as the emblem, the 'lively image', of Hieronimo's sorrow is a
somewhat 'literary' device, part of that self-conscious patterning that
spans the whole tragedy. But Hieronimo's encounter with him
provides an opportunity for the expression of genuine unforced
emotion, and Kyd shows that he possesses the theatrical tact to take
advantage of it. The character of Hieronimo, and especially his
soliloquies, provided not only theatre-experience so vivid, and so
popularly successful, that later dramatists were forced, almost in
self-defence, to write parodies of them; they also provided the
growth-points for a whole generation of tragic heroes and of tragic
verse.

To speak of Hieronimo as a fully-realised character is perhaps to
misrepresent the reality of Kyd's play. *The Spanish Tragedy* stands at
the turning-point between a drama of statement and a drama of
experience (or exploration), and Hieronimo remains largely a typical
rather than an individual figure: the lamenting father, and wily
avenger. Characterisation of the other persons is both slighter,
emotionally, and, in one or two cases, more helpful to the actor. The
Spanish king and the viceroy of Portugal, it is true, remain figure-
heads; Isabella utters a few speeches of lament and protest without

[27] The speech is fully and perceptively analysed in Clemen, op. cit., pp.
270–5.

becoming any more than a mouthpiece for lament and protest. Bel-imperia, on the contrary, appears as a woman with definite characteristics. Consider, for example, how freely her nature emerges during Kyd's masterly re-handling of the Senecan device of sticho-mythia (line-by-line dialogue), a device utterly dead in the hands of earlier and contemporary playwrights:

> LORENZO
> Sister, what means this melancholy walk?
> BEL-IMPERIA
> That for a while I wish no company.
> LORENZO
> But here the prince is come to visit you.
> BEL-IMPERIA
> That argues that he lives in liberty.
> BALTHAZAR
> No madam, but in pleasing servitude.
> BEL-IMPERIA
> Your prison then belike is your conceit.
>
> (I, iv, 77–82)

The excellence of this does not lie in any of the elaborately decorated verbal schemes we normally associate with Kyd, but rather in a sparseness that gives the actor ample opportunity. Again a much longer passage should be read to drive the point home. Bel-imperia's icy reserve, her barely-veiled hatred of Balthazar, comes across sharply in the stilted, glacially-polite exchange. Her formidable qualities emerge even more clearly as she confronts Lorenzo and Balthazar after her release from confinement (III, x, 24ff.); her protests are only less vigorous than the sardonic double-talk she offers in pretended acceptance of their explanations. No actress need have difficulty in playing Bel-imperia as a strong-willed—and sensually-inclined—woman.[28] Lorenzo, important as the first (certainly among the first) of a line of stage-Machiavels who exploited and furthered the Elizabethan delight in guile, nevertheless remains a more conventional character than his sister. Yet he is a dis-tinctly playable figure, astute, self-willed and slippery. His companion Balthazar is more thoroughly characterised, a rather ineffectual young man, deeply conscious (see II, i, 118–33) of his inferiority to Horatio. And his feelings of inferiority register themselves in his language; as Clemen has pointed out, his repetitive style of utter-ance, and his tedious dependence on rhetorical figures, 'is exactly in keeping with the irresolute, dependent, puppet-like role' he fills. His antagonist Horatio suffers from being the ideal young man, per-fectly adapted to becoming victim of a horrid murder; yet while he

[28] See II, iv, 20ff.; and see the note at ll. 45–9.

lives he does at least engage with Bel-imperia in sufficiently lively, and sufficiently sex-conscious, dialogue to show that he is no prig. And his love-poetry is, at the lowest, better than Balthazar's. The other figures in the tragedy are largely supporting cast without distinct characterisation.

The Spanish Tragedy has too often been discussed for its historic significance, too often plundered for the first example of this or that device; and above all, too often regarded merely as an example of a dead or moribund tradition, the mine where. Senecan device and rhetorical figure could be first quarried and then docketed. What is most remarkable in fact is not Kyd's debt to the past nor even what his play holds for development in the future by others, but the extent to which it is already a moving, successful stage-play in its own right. More noticeable than the display of academically-correct rhetorical devices is the extraordinary range of dramatic styles Kyd employs, from the most elaborate and artificial to the simplest and most economical. More significant than the borrowed Senecan plot-devices, like the Ghost and Revenge, is the swift and sure way in which Kyd communicates necessary information, in the early scenes especially; the play moves forward most boldly and satisfyingly. Above all, perhaps, *The Spanish Tragedy* is remarkable for the astonishingly deft and complete way in which Kyd has transmuted his theme into drama, by way of the intricate tactics of his play's structure. It would indeed be satisfying to see the tragedy well produced, though the production would almost certainly have to be in the hands of one of the great professional companies, for the conventions of Kyd's play, and the demands it makes on an actor's resources of voice and gesture, are well beyond the range of most amateurs. On the stage *The Spanish Tragedy* could I believe be shown to deserve its place as one of the first important English tragedies.[29]

[29] Peter B. Murray, *Thomas Kyd*, New York, 1969, emphasises the 'bizarre and almost comic rather than tragic tone' of most of the play; he adds that 'Elizabethan drama usually mingles the comic and the tragic, but only in this type initiated by Kyd is there often a true union of the two in an aesthetic whole'.

THE 'ADDITIONS'

The so-called 'Additions' to *The Spanish Tragedy* are grouped at the end of the present text. First printed in 1602 and there incorporated into the original text of the play, they comprise in all some 320 lines. Of the five additional passages, the first, second and fifth are brief and of slight importance; the third is a more sustained and accomplished piece, and the fourth is the well-known Painter scene, which amplifies in a striking manner the theme of Hieronimo's grief, and provides a remarkable opportunity for an actor to portray madness. Despite the excellence of some of the writing, however, there can be little doubt that inclusion of these scenes in an acting version would have the effect of upsetting the rhythm of Kyd's play.

It is most unlikely in fact that the 1602 text, including the 'Additions', was ever performed in its existing state. It is, for one thing, exceptionally long. It is more likely that the additional passages were intended to replace parts of Kyd's text which were felt by 1602 to be either old-fashioned or weak. Pavier, the publisher of this new edition, may have received from the theatre or from some intermediary, authorised or not, portions of the new copy; he would then incorporate them as best he could into an example of *1592*. Some support for this theory comes from the rough, or at the least 'free', state of the verse in the additional passages; we may suspect that some kind of printer's bungling has taken place.

The author of the 'Additions' is unknown. Ben Jonson was, we know, paid for revisions to *The Spanish Tragedy*, but those we have are rather unlike his characteristic work, and there are problems (of dating mainly) about connecting Henslowe's payment to Jonson with the printing of *1602*. Jonson, it is true, may have adapted his style to suit the play he was editing; but equally plausible is the suggestion that the lines are the work of another author, and that Jonson's revision of the play has unfortunately never reached print. Webster, Shakespeare and Dekker are among writers suggested as alternative authors, but the case for any one of them, or for other contemporaries, is not a strong one.

NOTE ON THE TEXT

The 1592 edition of *The Spanish Tragedy* is undated; it has been accepted as an octavo-in-fours of that year on the evidence of a dispute over the ownership of copyright. The dispute was settled by the Stationers' Company on 18 December 1592, when the publisher of *1592*, Edward White, was fined by the Company for 'having printed the spanishe tragedie belonging to Abell Ieffes'. There seems little doubt that printing took place earlier the same year.

1592 is the sole authoritative text of the play, and has of course been used as the basis of the present edition. The 'Additions' were first printed in quarto in 1602, a printing which serves as copy-text for the 'Additions' as given here. Other early editions, printed in 1594, 1599, 1603, 1610, 1615, 1618, 1623, 1633, testify to the play's enormous and long-lived popularity. Modern editions include those by Boas (*Works of Thomas Kyd*, 1901), McIlwraith (in *Five Elizabethan Tragedies*, 1938), Schick (*The Temple Dramatists*, 1898), Edwards (*The Revels Plays*, 1959), Joseph (*The New Mermaids*, 1964), Cairncross (*Regents Renaissance Drama Series*, 1967), and Ross (*The Fountainwell Drama Texts*, 1968). All of these have been used in the preparation of the present edition, but the text has been established and checked by a fresh collation of the British Museum copies of *1592* and *1602*.

Philip Edwards has argued, ingeniously and for the most part persuasively, that copy for *1592* included material of two distinct kinds, one taking the play as far as III, xiv, the other affecting the remaining scenes. Over the first section the text is a good one, showing little corruption and presenting few problems to the editor; the latter section contains some limited areas of corruption, irregularity and inconsistency. Writing of this second section, Edwards (p. xl) argues that 'the inconsistency in the action, which relates to the play-within-the-play and to Hieronimo's behaviour just before his death, may suggest that the text contains elements of a revised and abridged version of the play'; he adds that the 'presence of one unusually corrupt scene (III, xv) may suggest the use of inferior copy' and postulates that this may be drawn from a now lost edition of the play containing an unauthorised and corrupt version of Kyd's text. Edwards's reasoning explains more convincingly than any other the noticeable difference between the early and late parts of the text, and helps to account for the difficulties attaching to presentation of the last scenes of the play.[30] In general, however, it is clear that *1592* derives from material of high authority, probably Kyd's own manuscript, and not a manuscript originating in the theatre, or one much altered or marked up by theatre-officials. In these circumstances, an editor will take care not to alter substantive readings in his copy-text without clear evidence of corruption.

In accordance with the policy of this series, departures from the copy-text in substantive readings are noted among the glossarial notes at the foot of the page; earlier editors, whether Elizabethan or more recent, are not acknowledged in these notes except under the general designation 'ed.' In matters of punctuation I have been guided by what I have taken to be the convenience of a modern reader, and by the wish to present a text an actor could readily use on stage. I have therefore lightened somewhat the punctuation of the original (which proved rather formal) by removing commas, by reducing colons to commas, and by excising a fairly large number of unnecessary full-stops. When meaning seemed obscure, however, and not just deliberately ambiguous, I have occasionally added punctuation in the hope of assisting a modern reader. When foreign languages are quoted I have, like other recent editors, produced a form of the language recognisable by present-day linguists, though there is no certainty that Kyd originally got these languages 'right' by modern standards. In the matter of explanatory notes I have erred on the side of generosity, especially in providing brief glosses; I recognise it is irritating to meet glosses one does not need, but it is infinitely more annoying to find an editor has assumed knowledge where none exists. The reader will see I have been especially persistent in glossing classical allusions. Speech prefixes and the names in stage directions have been modernised and regularised throughout.

[30] See also the note at IV, iv, 165–7 and 179–82.

FURTHER READING

Arthur Freeman, *Thomas Kyd: Facts and Problems* (Oxford, 1967).

G. K. Hunter, 'Ironies of Justice in *The Spanish Tragedy*', *Renaissance Drama*, VIII (1965), 89–104.

Ejner J. Jensen, 'Kyd's *Spanish Tragedy*: The Play Explains Itself', *JEGP*, LXIV (1965), 7–16.

S. F. Johnson, '*The Spanish Tragedy*, or Babylon Revisited', in *Essays on Shakespeare and Elizabethan Drama in Honour of Hardin Craig*, ed. Richard Hosley (London, 1963), pp. 23–36.

T. S. Eliot, 'Seneca in Elizabethan Translation', *Selected Essays* (London, 1932), pp. 65–108.

Jonas A. Barish, '*The Spanish Tragedy*, or The Pleasures and Perils of Rhetoric', in *Elizabethan Theatre*, Stratford-upon-Avon Studies 9, ed. J. R. Brown and B. A. Harris (London, 1966), pp. 59–86.

John D. Ratliff, 'Hieronimo Explains Himself', *SP*, 54 (1957), 112–18.

M. C. Bradbrook, *Themes and Conventions of Elizabethan Tragedy* (London, 1935).

Wolfgang Clemen, *English Tragedy before Shakespeare* (London, 1961), pp. 100–12; 267–77.

Fredson T. Bowers, *Elizabethan Revenge Tragedy* (Princeton, 1940), chs. 1–3.

T. B. Tomlinson, *A Study of Elizabethan and Jacobean Tragedy* (Melbourne and Cambridge, 1964), ch. IV.

Peter B. Murray, *Thomas Kyd* (New York, 1969).

Philip Edwards, *Thomas Kyd and Early Elizabethan Tragedy* (London, 1966).

THE

SPANISH TRAGE-
die, Containing the lamentable
end of *Don Horatio*, and *Bel-imperia*:
with the pittifull death of
olde *Hieronimo*.

Newly corrected and amended of such grosse faults as
passed in the first impression.

AT LONDON
Printed by *Edward Allde*, for
Edward White.

[DRAMATIS PERSONAE

GHOST OF ANDREA
REVENGE
KING OF SPAIN
CYPRIAN, DUKE OF CASTILE, *his brother*
LORENZO, *the Duke's son*
BEL-IMPERIA, *Lorenzo's sister*
GENERAL *of the Spanish Army*

VICEROY OF PORTUGAL
PEDRO, *his brother*
BALTHAZAR, *his son*
ALEXANDRO ⎫ *Portuguese noblemen*
VILLUPPO ⎭
AMBASSADOR *of Portugal*

HIERONIMO, *Knight Marshal of Spain*
ISABELLA, *his wife*
HORATIO, *their son*

PEDRINGANO, *servant to Bel-imperia*
SERBERINE, *servant to Balthazar*
CHRISTOPHIL, *servant to Lorenzo*
BAZULTO, *an old man*

Page *to Lorenzo*, Three Watchmen, Messenger, Deputy, Hangman, Maid *to Isabella*, Two Portuguese, Servant, Three Citizens, Portuguese Nobles, Soldiers, Officers, Attendants, Halberdiers

Three Knights, Three Kings, a Drummer *in the first Dumb-show*, Hymen, Two Torch-bearers *in the second Dumb-show*

In the 'Additions':
PEDRO ⎫ *Hieronimo's servants*
JAQUES ⎭
BAZARDO, *a Painter*]

3

THE SPANISH TRAGEDY

Act I, Scene i

Enter the Ghost of ANDREA, *and with him* REVENGE

ANDREA

When this eternal substance of my soul
Did live imprisoned in my wanton flesh,
Each in their function serving other's need,
I was a courtier in the Spanish court.
My name was Don Andrea, my descent,   5
Though not ignoble, yet inferior far
To gracious fortunes of my tender youth:
For there in prime and pride of all my years,
By duteous service and deserving love,
In secret I possessed a worthy dame,   10
Which hight sweet Bel-imperia by name.
But in the harvest of my summer joys
Death's winter nipped the blossoms of my bliss,
Forcing divorce betwixt my love and me.
For in the late conflict with Portingale   15
My valour drew me into danger's mouth,
Till life to death made passage through my wounds.

8 *prime* spring-time
8 *pride* the most flourishing condition (*O.E.D.*)
10 *possessed* made love to
11 *hight* was called
13 *nipped* destroyed by frost
14 *divorce* separation
15 *Portingale* Portugal

1 ff. These opening lines were often parodied in later Elizabethan plays.
Edwards quotes Beaumont's *The Knight of the Burning Pestle* (first
performed 1607), V, i: 'When I was mortal, this my costive corpse/Did
lap up figs and raisins in the Strand.'
10-11 *In secret . . . by name* The details of this intrigue are never made
plain, perhaps to avoid an unfavourable estimate of Bel-imperia.
It is, however, mentioned again at II, i, 45-8, III, x, 54-5 and III,
xiv, 111-12. Its clandestine nature anticipates the Horatio / Bel-imperia
relationship, making for one more parallel between Andrea and Horatio.

When I was slain, my soul descended straight
To pass the flowing stream of Acheron:
But churlish Charon, only boatman there,   20
Said that my rites of burial not performed,
I might not sit amongst his passengers.
Ere Sol had slept three nights in Thetis' lap
And slaked his smoking chariot in her flood,
By Don Horatio, our Knight Marshal's son,   25
My funerals and obsequies were done.
Then was the ferryman of hell content
To pass me over to the slimy strond,
That leads to fell Avernus' ugly waves:
There, pleasing Cerberus with honeyed speech,   30
I passed the perils of the foremost porch.
Not far from hence, amidst ten thousand souls,
Sat Minos, Aeacus, and Rhadamanth,
To whom no sooner 'gan I make approach,
To crave a passport for my wandering ghost,   35

19 *Acheron* a river of the lower world, identified here with Styx
   where Charon was ferryman
23 *Sol* the sun
23 *Thetis* daughter of Nereus, a Homeric sea-god; here, the sea
24 *slaked* extinguished the flame of
24 *her flood* the sea
28 *strond* shore
29 *fell* cruel, deadly
29 *Avernus* the lake near Puteoli thought to serve as entrance to the
   underworld
30 *Cerberus* the monstrous three-headed dog, guardian of the underworld
31 *porch* place of entry
33 *Minos, Aeacus, Rhadamanth* judges of the underworld
35 *passport* safe-conduct, letters of protection

18 ff. This description of the underworld derives from *Aeneid* book VI,
   though Kyd has altered the details of Vergil's description. For a full
   discussion see Boas, pp. 394-5.
25 *Knight Marshal* a legal official of the English royal household 'who
   had judicial cognizance of transgressions "within the king's house and
   verge", i.e. within a radius of twelve miles from the king's palace'
   (*O.E.D.*, Marshal sb. 6b). Hieronimo's judicial responsibilities are
   insisted upon even before Horatio's murder.

But Minos, in graven leaves of lottery,
Drew forth the manner of my life and death.
'This knight,' quoth he, 'both lived and died in love,
And for his love tried fortune of the wars,
And by war's fortune lost both love and life.'   40
'Why then,' said Aeacus, 'convey him hence,
To walk with lovers in our fields of love,
And spend the course of everlasting time
Under green myrtle trees and cypress shades.'
'No, no,' said Rhadamanth, 'it were not well   45
With loving souls to place a martialist:
He died in war, and must to martial fields,
Where wounded Hector lives in lasting pain,
And Achilles' Myrmidons do scour the plain.'
Then Minos, mildest censor of the three,   50
Made this device to end the difference:
'Send him,' quoth he, 'to our infernal king,
To doom him as best seems his majesty.'
To this effect my passport straight was drawn.
In keeping on my way to Pluto's court,   55
Through dreadful shades of ever-glooming night,
I saw more sights than thousand tongues can tell,
Or pens can write, or mortal hearts can think.
Three ways there were: that on the right-hand side
Was ready way unto the foresaid fields   60
Where lovers live and bloody martialists,
But either sort contained within his bounds.

46 *martialist* warrior
49 *Achilles' Myrmidons* followers of the warrior Achilles in Homer;
   killers of Hector (l.48)
49 *scour* range speedily over
50 *censor* judge
52 *infernal* underworld
53 *doom* give judgment on
55 *Pluto* king of the underworld
56 *ever-glooming* always dark and threatening
62 *his* its own

36 *graven leaves of lottery* not clear. Lots are drawn in Vergil to settle
   where the dead will spend the after-life, but here it seems that
   Minos is, additionally, reading from some account of Andrea's past.
   Edwards comments: '*Drew forth* (l.37) is best interpreted literally and
   we must suppose that Minos draws from his urn the lottery slip on
   which was engraved the manner of life which Andrea has by now
   fulfilled, i.e., what has been his lot'.

The left-hand path, declining fearfully,
Was ready downfall to the deepest hell,
Where bloody Furies shakes their whips of steel,   65
And poor Ixion turns an endless wheel;
Where usurers are choked with melting gold,
And wantons are embraced with ugly snakes,
And murderers groan with never-killing wounds,
And perjured wights scalded in boiling lead,   70
And all foul sins with torments overwhelmed.
'Twixt these two ways I trod the middle path,
Which brought me to the fair Elysian green,
In midst whereof there stands a stately tower,
The walls of brass, the gates of adamant.   75
Here finding Pluto with his Proserpine,
I showed my passport, humbled on my knee;
Whereat fair Proserpine began to smile,
And begged that only she might give my doom.
Pluto was pleased, and sealed it with a kiss.   80
Forthwith, Revenge, she rounded thee in th'ear,
And bade thee lead me through the gates of horn,
Where dreams have passage in the silent night.

63 *declining* sloping down
64 *downfall* precipice, gulf
65 *Furies* mythical avengers of crime
66 *Ixion* punished on a treadmill for seeking Hera's love
70 *wights* persons
73 *Elysian green* Elysium is the abode of the blessed in the after-life;
    Vergil places it in the underworld
75 *adamant* very hard stone; diamond
76 *Proserpine* the Greek Persephone, consort of Dis (or Pluto),
    queen of the underworld
77 *humbled on my knee* kneeling in humility
79 *doom* sentence
81 *rounded* whispered
82 *horn* ed. (Hor: *1592*)

63–71 Lorenzo and his confederates are doomed to this region of hell at
    the play's end, while Horatio, Bel-imperia and Hieronimo take the
    alternative path (for lovers and martialists). See IV, v, 17 ff.
82 *gates of horn* The gate of horn in *Aeneid* VI (modelled on Homer)
    is the gate through which *true* dreams or visions pass, as against the
    ivory gate of *false* dreams; a prediction that the purposes of Revenge
    will be fulfilled.

No sooner had she spoke but we were here,
I wot not how, in twinkling of an eye.   85
REVENGE
Then know, Andrea, that thou art arrived
Where thou shalt see the author of thy death,
Don Balthazar, the prince of Portingale,
Deprived of life by Bel-imperia.
Here sit we down to see the mystery,   90
And serve for Chorus in this tragedy.

Act I, Scene ii

Enter SPANISH KING, GENERAL, CASTILE, HIERONIMO

KING
Now say, Lord General, how fares our camp?
GENERAL
All well, my sovereign liege, except some few
That are deceased by fortune of the war.
KING
But what portends thy cheerful countenance,
And posting to our presence thus in haste?   5
Speak man, hath fortune given us victory?
GENERAL
Victory, my liege, and that with little loss.
KING
Our Portingals will pay us tribute then?
GENERAL
Tribute and wonted homage therewithal.
KING
Then blest be heaven, and guider of the heavens,   10
From whose fair influence such justice flows.

85 *wot* know
90 *mystery* events yet to be revealed, of a special significance
 1 *camp* army in the field
 5 *posting* speeding
 8 *Portingals* Portuguese
 8 *tribute* tribute-money

86–9 The audience's knowledge that these events will take place has an
      important bearing on their attitude to the action and the characters in the
      main play.
 1–21 The opening lines of this scene have a calculated air of light
      optimism and even complacency: ironic in view of our knowledge
      that catastrophe is to follow.

CASTILE
> *O multum dilecte Deo, tibi militat aether,*
> *Et conjuratae curvato poplite gentes*
> *Succumbunt: recti soror est victoria juris.*

KING
Thanks to my loving brother of Castile.   15
But General, unfold in brief discourse
Your form of battle and your war's success,
That adding all the pleasure of thy news
Unto the height of former happiness,
With deeper wage and greater dignity   20
We may reward thy blissful chivalry.

GENERAL
Where Spain and Portingale do jointly knit
Their frontiers, leaning on each other's bound,
There met our armies in their proud array:
Both furnished well, both full of hope and fear,   25
Both menacing alike with daring shows,
Both vaunting sundry colours of device,
Both cheerly sounding trumpets, drums and fifes,
Both raising dreadful clamours to the sky,
That valleys, hills, and rivers made rebound,   30
And heaven itself was frighted with the sound.
Our battles both were pitched in squadron form,

13 *poplite* ed. (*poplito 1592*)
16 *unfold* explain
20 *deeper wage* richer reward
21 *chivalry* skill in arms
23 *bound* boundary
25 *furnished* equipped
27 *vaunting* displaying proudly
27 *colours of device* heraldic banners
32 *battles* forces
32 *squadron form* in a square formation

12–14 'O one much loved of God, for thee the heavens contend, and the
united peoples fall down on bended knee: victory is sister to just
rights.' Boas indicates the lines are adapted from Claudian's *De Tertio
Consulatu Honorii*, 96–8.

22–84 The General's account of the battle (in accordance with Kyd's
narrative patterning) expands that of Andrea at I, i, 15 ff., and anticipates both the distorted version by Villuppo (I, iii, 59 ff.) and Horatio's
corrective account at I, iv, 9 ff. It serves both as 'good theatre' in the
elaborate theatrical vein enjoyed by Elizabethans, and also to establish
an unbiased perspective on events from which the rest of the plot
springs.

Each corner strongly fenced with wings of shot;
But ere we joined and came to push of pike,
I brought a squadron of our readiest shot   35
From out our rearward to begin the fight:
They brought another wing to encounter us.
Meanwhile, our ordnance played on either side,
And captains strove to have their valours tried.
Don Pedro, their chief horsemen's colonel,   40
Did with his cornet bravely make attempt
To break the order of our battle ranks:
But Don Rogero, worthy man of war,
Marched forth against him with our musketeers,
And stopped the malice of his fell approach.   45
While they maintain hot skirmish to and fro,
Both battles join and fall to handy blows,
Their violent shot resembling th'ocean's rage,
When, roaring loud, and with a swelling tide,
It beats upon the rampiers of huge rocks,   50
And gapes to swallow neighbour-bounding lands.
Now while Bellona rageth here and there,
Thick storms of bullets rain like winter's hail,
And shivered lances dark the troubled air.
       Pede pes et cuspide cuspis;   55
   Arma sonant armis, vir petiturque viro.

33 *fenced* defended, reinforced
33 *wings of shot* soldiers carrying firearms placed on the outer edges
    of the formation
34 *push of pike* hand-to-hand fighting
38 *ordnance* ed. (ordinance *1592*) heavy artillery
38 *played* directed their fire
40 *colonel* ed. (Corlonell *1592*) three syllables
41 *cornet* a squadron of cavalry
45 *malice* danger, harm
47 *handy* hand-to-hand
48 *shot* shooting, exchange of fire (presumably at close quarters)
50 *rampiers* ramparts
51 *neighbour-bounding* neighbouring, on its margin
52 *Bellona* Roman goddess of war
53 *rain* ed. (ran *1592*)   54 *dark* darken
56 *Arma* ed. (*Anni 1592*)   56 *armis* ed. (*annis 1592*)

55–6 'Foot against foot and spear against spear, arms ring on arms and
    man is assailed by man.' Boas says the Latin is taken partly from
    Statius (*Thebais*, viii. 399) and, quoting Schick, partly structured on
    analogies in Vergil and Curtius.

On every side drop captains to the ground,
And soldiers, some ill-maimed, some slain outright:
Here falls a body scindered from his head,
There legs and arms lie bleeding on the grass,   60
Mingled with weapons and unbowelled steeds,
That scattering overspread the purple plain.
In all this turmoil, three long hours and more,
The victory to neither part inclined,
Till Don Andrea with his brave lanciers   65
In their main battle made so great a breach
That, half dismayed, the multitude retired:
But Balthazar, the Portingales' young prince,
Brought rescue, and encouraged them to stay.
Here-hence the fight was eagerly renewed,   70
And in that conflict was Andrea slain—
Brave man at arms, but weak to Balthazar.
Yet while the prince, insulting over him,
Breathed out proud vaunts, sounding to our reproach,
Friendship and hardy valour joined in one   75
Pricked forth Horatio, our Knight Marshal's son,
To challenge forth that prince in single fight.
Not long between these twain the fight endured,
But straight the prince was beaten from his horse,
And forced to yield him prisoner to his foe: 80
When he was taken, all the rest they fled,
And our carbines pursued them to the death,

58 *ill-maimed* badly injured
59 *scindered* sundered
62 *purple* blood-red, covered in blood
65 *lanciers* (two syllables) lancers
70 *Here-hence* as a result of this (*O.E.D.*, 1)
72 *man at arms* specifically, a mounted soldier
73 *insulting* exulting
74 *sounding to* tending to, inferring (*O.E.D.*, 5a)
76 *Pricked forth* spurred on
80 *him* himself
82 *carbines* presumably soldiers carrying these weapons (*O.E.D.* has no example)

72 A reminiscence, in keeping with the heroic manner of these lines, of references to defeated warriors in Homer.

Till, Phoebus waning to the western deep,
Our trumpeters were charged to sound retreat.

KING

Thanks good Lord General for these good news;   85
And for some argument of more to come,
Take this and wear it for thy sovereign's sake.

Give him his chain

But tell me now, hast thou confirmed a peace?

GENERAL

No peace, my liege, but peace conditional,
That if with homage tribute be well paid,   90
The fury of your forces will be stayed:
And to this peace their viceroy hath subscribed,

Give the KING *a paper*

And made a solemn vow that, during life,
His tribute shall be truly paid to Spain.

KING

These words, these deeds, become thy person well.   95
But now, Knight Marshal, frolic with thy king,
For 'tis thy son that wins this battle's prize.

HIERONIMO

Long may he live to serve my sovereign liege,
And soon decay unless he serve my liege.

A tucket afar off

KING

Nor thou, nor he, shall die without reward.   100
What means the warning of this trumpet's sound?

GENERAL

This tells me that your grace's men of war,
Such as war's fortune hath reserved from death,
Come marching on towards your royal seat,
To show themselves before your majesty,   105
For so I gave in charge at my depart.
Whereby by demonstration shall appear,

83 *Phoebus* the sun
83 *waning* ed. (wauing *1592*)
83 *deep* the sea
86 *argument* token
89 *but* except
91 *stayed* restrained, halted
92 *subscribed* signed his name
96 *frolic* rejoice, be happy
99 *decay* fail in health and fortune
101 *the* ed. (this *1592*)

That all (except three hundred or few more)
Are safe returned and by their foes enriched.

The Army enters; BALTHAZAR, *between* LORENZO *and* HORATIO,
captive

KING
A gladsome sight! I long to see them here.   110
                              They enter and pass by
Was that the warlike prince of Portingale,
That by our nephew was in triumph led?
GENERAL
It was, my liege, the prince of Portingale.
KING
But what was he that on the other side
Held him by th'arm as partner of the prize?   115
HIERONIMO
That was my son, my gracious sovereign,
Of whom, though from his tender infancy
My loving thoughts did never hope but well,
He never pleased his father's eyes till now,
Nor filled my heart with overcloying joys.   120
KING
Go let them march once more about these walls,
That staying them we may confer and talk
With our brave prisoner and his double guard.
Hieronimo, it greatly pleaseth us,
That in our victory thou have a share,   125
By virtue of thy worthy son's exploit.
                              Enter [the Army] again
Bring hither the young prince of Portingale:
The rest march on, but ere they be dismissed,

120 *overcloying* causing surfeit, satiating
122 *staying* stopping

---

108 This calm writing-off of 300 men perhaps underlines what we know
    to be the false complacency of the Spanish court. Compare the opening
    speeches of *Much Ado*.
109 s.d. The double entry of the army (here and after 1.126) complements
    the high verbal flourish of the General's speech and extends the air of
    martial grandeur and confidence; it also permits the theatrical display
    so dear to Elizabethans.
111 ff. Kyd's very strong sense of dramatic structure brings the three princi-
    pal antagonists together at their first entry; the later enmity between
    Lorenzo and Horatio is visually suggested by each laying claim to the
    prisoner Balthazar.

We will bestow on every soldier
Two ducats, and on every leader ten,   130
That they may know our largess welcomes them.
    Exeunt all [the Army] but BALTHAZAR, LORENZO, HORATIO
Welcome, Don Balthazar, welcome, nephew,
And thou, Horatio, thou art welcome too.
Young prince, although thy father's hard misdeeds,
In keeping back the tribute that he owes,   135
Deserve but evil measure at our hands,
Yet shalt thou know that Spain is honourable.

BALTHAZAR
The trespass that my father made in peace
Is now controlled by fortune of the wars;
And cards once dealt, it boots not ask why so.   140
His men are slain, a weakening to his realm,
His colours seized, a blot unto his name,
His son distressed, a corsive to his heart:
These punishments may clear his late offence.

KING
Ay, Balthazar, if he observe this truce,   145
Our peace will grow the stronger for these wars.
Meanwhile live thou, though not in liberty,
Yet free from bearing any servile yoke;
For in our hearing thy deserts were great,
And in our sight thyself art gracious.   150

BALTHAZAR
And I shall study to deserve this grace.

KING
But tell me, for their holding makes me doubt,
To which of these twain art thou prisoner?

129–31 (lineation ed. We . . . ducats / And . . . know / Our . . them
    1592)
131 *largess* money and gifts bestowed by a king
139 *controlled* brought to an end
140 *boots* profits   142 *colours* standards, flags
143 *distressed* taken prisoner
143 *corsive* corrosive (a destructive substance)
144 *clear* erase   144 *late* previous, past
152 *their holding* the way they hold you

152 ff. Clemen (p. 101) points out that the scene from this point corre-
    sponds to the familiar Elizabethan 'tribunal scene' in which a dispute
    between two nobles is arbitrated by the king. (Compare e.g. *Richard II*,
    I, i.) Kyd's handling of this conventional situation is much more
    flexible dramatically than that of his predecessors.

LORENZO

  To me, my liege.

HORATIO   To me, my sovereign.

LORENZO

  This hand first took his courser by the reins.   155

HORATIO

  But first my lance did put him from his horse.

LORENZO

  I seized his weapon, and enjoyed it first.

HORATIO

  But first I forced him lay his weapons down.

KING

  Let go his arm, upon our privilege.   *[They] let him go*

  Say, worthy prince, to whether didst thou yield?   160

BALTHAZAR

  To him in courtesy, to this perforce:

  He spake me fair, this other gave me strokes;

  He promised life, this other threatened death;

  He wan my love, this other conquered me;

  And truth to say I yield myself to both.   165

HIERONIMO

  But that I know your grace for just and wise,

  And might seem partial in this difference,

  Enforced by nature and by law of arms

  My tongue should plead for young Horatio's right.

  He hunted well that was a lion's death,   170

  Not he that in a garment wore his skin:

  So hares may pull dead lions by the beard.

KING

  Content thee, Marshal, thou shalt have no wrong;

  And for thy sake thy son shall want no right.

  Will both abide the censure of my doom?   175

LORENZO

  I crave no better than your grace awards.

159 *privilege* the king's prerogative
160 *whether* which of the two
164 *wan* won
167 *partial* guilty of favouritism
175 *censure of my doom* the outcome of my judgment

170–2 Hieronimo argues that Horatio deserves credit as the true con-
    queror of Balthazar. The reference in l.171 derives, as Edwards shows,
    from the Fourth Fable of Avian concerning an ass who disports him-
    self in a lion's skin he has found. Line 172 is proverbial; even timid hares
    may beard a *dead* lion.

HORATIO
  Nor I, although I sit beside my right.
KING
  Then by my judgment thus your strife shall end:
  You both deserve and both shall have reward.
  Nephew, thou took'st his weapon and his horse,   180
  His weapons and his horse are thy reward.
  Horatio, thou didst force him first to yield,
  His ransom therefore is thy valour's fee:
  Appoint the sum as you shall both agree.
  But nephew, thou shalt have the prince in guard,   185
  For thine estate best fitteth such a guest:
  Horatio's house were small for all his train.
  Yet in regard thy substance passeth his,
  And that just guerdon may befall desert,
  To him we yield the armour of the prince.   190
  How likes Don Balthazar of this device?
BALTHAZAR
  Right well my liege, if this proviso were,
  That Don Horatio bear us company,
  Whom I admire and love for chivalry.
KING
  Horatio, leave him not that loves thee so.   195
  Now let us hence to see our soldiers paid,
  And feast our prisoner as our friendly guest.   *Exeunt*

Act I, Scene iii

Enter VICEROY, ALEXANDRO, VILLUPPO [, *Attendants*]

VICEROY
  Is our ambassador despatched for Spain?
ALEXANDRO
  Two days, my liege, are passed since his depart.
VICEROY
  And tribute payment gone along with him?

---

177 *sit beside* forgo (Edwards)   188 *in regard* since
189 *that* in order that
189 *guerdon* reward
190 *him* Horatio

---

187 Horatio's social standing (like Hieronimo's) is emphatically lower
    than that of Lorenzo and Bel-imperia (and of course Balthazar).
    See also II, iv, 61 and III, x, 57.

ALEXANDRO
  Ay my good lord.
VICEROY
  Then rest we here awhile in our unrest,   5
  And feed our sorrows with some inward sighs,
  For deepest cares break never into tears.
  But wherefore sit I in a regal throne?
  This better fits a wretch's endless moan.

                                Falls to the ground
  Yet this is higher than my fortunes reach,   10
  And therefore better than my state deserves.
  Ay, ay, this earth, image of melancholy,
  Seeks him whom fates adjudge to misery:
  Here let me lie, now am I at the lowest.
    Qui jacet in terra, non habet unde cadat.   15
    In me consumpsit vires fortuna nocendo,
    Nil superest ut jam possit obesse magis.
  Yes, Fortune may bereave me of my crown:
  Here, take it now; let Fortune do her worst,
  She will not rob me of this sable weed: 20
  O no, she envies none but pleasant things.
  Such is the folly of despiteful chance!
  Fortune is blind and sees not my deserts,
  So is she deaf and hears not my laments:

9 s.d. follows l.11 in *1592*
10 'My circumstances are even worse than this suggests.'
11 *state* condition, situation
20 *sable weed* black costume
21 *envies* feels ill-will towards
22 *despiteful* malicious

---

5 ff. The Viceroy's speech contrasts with the self-congratulation of the
  Spanish King, and anticipates Hieronimo's similar grief over the loss
  of a son. Clemen (p. 269) draws attention to Kyd's dramatically-alert
  transformation in these lines of the standard 'lament speech'. Compare
  the King's lines in *Richard II*, III, ii, 144 ff.
12 *image of melancholy* Melancholy is the bodily 'humour' (responsible for a
  person's temperament) that corresponds to the element earth, one of
  the four elements (the others are air, fire and water) that make up all
  created things.
15–17 'If one lies on the ground, one has no further to fall. Towards me
  Fortune has exhausted her power to injure; there is nothing further
  that can happen to me.' The first line is borrowed from Alanus de
  Insulis, *Lib. Parab.*, cap. 2, l.19, the second from Seneca's *Agamemnon*
  l.698, while the third is probably Kyd's own composition. (See W. P.
  Mustard, *PQ*, V (1926), 85–6.)

And could she hear, yet is she wilful mad,   25
And therefore will not pity my distress.
Suppose that she could pity me, what then?
What help can be expected at her hands,
Whose foot is standing on a rolling stone,
And mind more mutable than fickle winds?   30
Why wail I then, where's hope of no redress?
O yes, complaining makes my grief seem less.
My late ambition hath distained my faith,
My breach of faith occasioned bloody wars,
Those bloody wars have spent my treasure,   35
And with my treasure my people's blood,
And with their blood, my joy and best beloved,
My best beloved, my sweet and only son.
O wherefore went I not to war myself?
The cause was mine, I might have died for both: 40
My years were mellow, his but young and green,
My death were natural, but his was forced.

ALEXANDRO
No doubt, my liege, but still the prince survives.
VICEROY
Survives! ay, where?
ALEXANDRO
In Spain, a prisoner by mischance of war.   45
VICEROY
Then they have slain him for his father's fault.
ALEXANDRO
That were a breach to common law of arms.

---

25 *wilful mad* deliberately closed to reason
29 *is* ed. (*not in 1592*)
30 *mutable* ever-changing
33 *distained* sullied
35, 36 *treasure* Edwards says tri-syllabic: 'treas-u-er'
42 *forced* against the course of nature
46 *fault* crime, wrongdoing

23–30 In the emblem books, Fortune is normally depicted as blind,
sometimes as deaf, and frequently as standing on a rolling sphere;
all to express her lack of discrimination and changeableness. The
Viceroy's complaint of Fortune contributes to the play's preoccupation
with justice and retribution. Lines 33-42 are the Viceroy's attempt to
construct a rational (and therefore 'just') explanation for what has
happened, and so to rationalise Fortune.

VICEROY
They reck no laws that meditate revenge.
ALEXANDRO
His ransom's worth will stay from foul revenge.
VICEROY
No, if he lived the news would soon be here.   50
ALEXANDRO
Nay, evil news fly faster still than good.
VICEROY
Tell me no more of news, for he is dead.
VILLUPPO
My sovereign, pardon the author of ill news,
And I'll bewray the fortune of thy son.
VICEROY
Speak on, I'll guerdon thee whate'er it be: 55
Mine ear is ready to receive ill news,
My heart grown hard 'gainst mischief's battery;
Stand up I say, and tell thy tale at large.
VILLUPPO
Then hear that truth which these mine eyes have seen.
When both the armies were in battle joined,   60
Don Balthazar, amidst the thickest troops,
To win renown did wondrous feats of arms:
Amongst the rest I saw him hand to hand
In single fight with their Lord General;
Till Alexandro, that here counterfeits   65
Under the colour of a duteous friend,
Discharged his pistol at the prince's back,
As though he would have slain their general.
But therewithal Don Balthazar fell down,
And when he fell, then we began to fly: 70
But had he lived, the day had sure been ours.

48 *reck* heed
49 *stay* restrain
53 *author* one who transmits; or one who lends his authority to,
   vouches for
54 *bewray* reveal
55 *guerdon* reward
57 *mischief* misfortune
66 *colour* pretence

48 That revenge was by nature lawless was the accepted Elizabethan
attitude (see Bowers, esp. pp. 3-14).

ALEXANDRO

  O wicked forgery! O traitorous miscreant!

VICEROY

  Hold thou thy peace! But now, Villuppo, say,
  Where then became the carcase of my son?

VILLUPPO

  I saw them drag it to the Spanish tents.   75

VICEROY

  Ay, ay, my nightly dreams have told me this.
  Thou false, unkind, unthankful, traitorous beast,
  Wherein had Balthazar offended thee,
  That thou shouldst thus betray him to our foes?
  Was't Spanish gold that bleared so thine eyes   80
  That thou couldst see no part of our deserts?
  Perchance because thou art Terceira's lord,
  Thou hadst some hope to wear this diadem,
  If first my son and then myself were slain:
  But thy ambitious thought shall break thy neck.   85
  Ay, this was it that made thee spill his blood,
              Take the crown and put it on again
  But I'll now wear it till thy blood be spilt.

ALEXANDRO

  Vouchsafe, dread sovereign, to hear me speak.

VICEROY

  Away with him, his sight is second hell;
  Keep him till we determine of his death.   90
            [Exeunt Attendants with ALEXANDRO]
  If Balthazar be dead, he shall not live.
  Villuppo, follow us for thy reward.   *Exit* VICEROY

VILLUPPO

  Thus have I with an envious, forged tale

72 *forgery* falsehood, fabrication
72 *miscreant* villain, rascal
83 *diadem* ed. (Diadome *1592*)
93 *envious* malicious

---

82 *Terceira's lord* Boas says that Alexandro was apparently *Capitão
  Donatario* of Terceira, an island in the Azores group, and would
  because of this position enjoy virtually despotic powers. The title was
  given to the first discoverers and colonisers of overseas territories and
  was hereditary.

93–5 The villain's explicit confession seems awkward to modern readers;
  it remained a convention widely acceptable in the Elizabethan theatre.
  Compare e.g. Flamineo in *The White Devil*, IV, ii, 242-6.

Deceived the king, betrayed mine enemy,
And hope for guerdon of my villainy.   *Exit*   95

Act I, Scene iv

Enter HORATIO *and* BEL-IMPERIA

BEL-IMPERIA

Signior Horatio, this is the place and hour
Wherein I must entreat thee to relate
The circumstance of Don Andrea's death,
Who, living, was my garland's sweetest flower,
And in his death hath buried my delights.   5

HORATIO

For love of him and service to yourself,
I nill refuse this heavy doleful charge.
Yet tears and sighs, I fear will hinder me.
When both our armies were enjoined in fight,
Your worthy chevalier amidst the thick'st,   10
For glorious cause still aiming at the fairest,
Was at the last by young Don Balthazar
Encountered hand to hand: their fight was long,
Their hearts were great, their clamours menacing,
Their strength alike, their strokes both dangerous.   15
But wrathful Nemesis, that wicked power,
Envying at Andrea's praise and worth,
Cut short his life, to end his praise and worth.
She, she herself, disguised in armour's mask,

7 *nill* will not
9 *enjoined* joined
10 *chevalier* a lady's cavalier or gallant
16 *Nemesis* the goddess of retribution, especially exercised by the gods
   against human presumption
17 *Envying at* regarding with ill-will

6–43 Horatio's account of the battle gives the personal angle, as against
   the General's more objective description. Contrast the emotionalism
   of many lines in this speech with the General's technicalities (esp.
   I, ii, 32 ff.).
11 'always aiming at the most outstanding achievements in honour of his
   glorious cause' (the love for Bel-imperia that inspired him).
19–20 Kyd probably refers to *Aeneid*, II, ll.615–16, as Boas suggests, but
   though Pallas (Athene) is there mentioned, it is Juno who is 'ferro
   accincta', 'girt with steel'.

(As Pallas was before proud Pergamus)   20
Brought in a fresh supply of halberdiers,
Which paunched his horse, and dinged him to the ground.
Then young Don Balthazar with ruthless rage,
Taking advantage of his foe's distress,
Did finish what his halberdiers begun,   25
And left not till Andrea's life was done.
Then, though too late, incensed with just remorse,
I with my band set forth against the prince,
And brought him prisoner from his halberdiers.

BEL-IMPERIA

Would thou hadst slain him that so slew my love.   30
But then was Don Andrea's carcase lost?

HORATIO

No, that was it for which I chiefly strove,
Nor stepped I back till I recovered him:
I took him up, and wound him in mine arms,
And welding him unto my private tent,   35
There laid him down, and dewed him with my tears,
And sighed and sorrowed as became a friend.
But neither friendly sorrow, sighs nor tears
Could win pale Death from his usurpéd right.
Yet this I did, and less I could not do: 40
I saw him honoured with due funeral.

20 *Pallas* Athene, patroness of Athens, and one of the divinities
    associated with the Greeks at Troy
20 *Pergamus* Troy
21 *halberdiers* soldiers carrying halberds, weapons that are a com-
    bination of spear and battle-axe, the head being mounted on a
    long pole
22 *paunched* stabbed in the belly
22 *dinged* thrust, struck
27 *just remorse* righteous indignation and pity
34 *wound* embraced
35 *welding* carrying

21–6 Andrea is overwhelmed by superior numbers, not killed in fair
    combat (see Bel-imperia's comment, ll.73–5). *I Hieronimo* also lays
    stress on the dishonourable way Balthazar brought about Andrea's
    death (scene xi; and see Cairncross, pp. xviii and 49).

This scarf I plucked from off his lifeless arm,
And wear it in remembrance of my friend.

BEL-IMPERIA

I know the scarf, would he had kept it still,
For had he lived he would have kept it still,   45
And worn it for his Bel-imperia's sake:
For 'twas my favour at his last depart.
But now wear thou it both for him and me,
For after him thou hast deserved it best.
But, for thy kindness in his life and death,   50
Be sure while Bel-imperia's life endures,
She will be Don Horatio's thankful friend.

HORATIO

And, madam, Don Horatio will not slack
Humbly to serve fair Bel-imperia.
But now, if your good liking stand thereto,   55
I'll crave your pardon to go seek the prince,
For so the duke your father gave me charge.   *Exit*

BEL-IMPERIA

Ay, go Horatio, leave me here alone,
For solitude best fits my cheerless mood.
Yet what avails to wail Andrea's death,   60
From whence Horatio proves my second love?
Had he not loved Andrea as he did,
He could not sit in Bel-imperia's thoughts.
But how can love find harbour in my breast,
Till I revenge the death of my beloved?   65

---

42 *lifeless* ed. (liveless *1592*)
47 *favour* a gift given to a lover to be worn as a token of affection

---

42 *This scarf* 'Scarves' or 'handkerchers' and sometimes gloves were
worn as ladies' favours (see l.47) by knights on the battlefield (compare
the 'pledges' Troilus and Cressida exchange: see *TC*, IV, iv and V, ii).
When Horatio wears the scarf (see ll.48, 49) he becomes visually
Andrea's representative; if this scarf is the 'bloody handkercher' that
Hieronimo takes from the dead Horatio's body (see II, v, 51 and III,
xiii, 86–9) then it also serves as a visual link between the twin revenges,
for Andrea and Horatio.

60–8 Bel-imperia's love for Horatio may strike us as sudden, unmotiv-
ated and even (ll.66–8) unpleasantly mixed with calculation. Partly
this is a matter of dramatic convention (the early plays were not greatly
concerned with psychological probability) and partly an item in Kyd's
developing portrait of Bel-imperia as a formidable woman, decisively
able to control and direct her emotions. Her decision is also of course
vital in joining the two revenges.

Yes, second love shall further my revenge.
I'll love Horatio, my Andrea's friend,
The more to spite the prince that wrought his end.
And where Don Balthazar, that slew my love,
Himself now pleads for favour at my hands,   70
He shall in rigour of my just disdain
Reap long repentance for his murderous deed.
For what was't else but murderous cowardice,
So many to oppress one valiant knight,
Without respect of honour in the fight?   75
And here he comes that murdered my delight.

Enter LORENZO *and* BALTHAZAR

LORENZO
Sister, what means this melancholy walk?
BEL-IMPERIA
That for a while I wish no company.
LORENZO
But here the prince is come to visit you.
BEL-IMPERIA
That argues that he lives in liberty.   80
BALTHAZAR
No madam, but in pleasing servitude.
BEL-IMPERIA
Your prison then belike is your conceit.
BALTHAZAR
Ay, by conceit my freedom is enthralled.
BEL-IMPERIA
Then with conceit enlarge yourself again.
BALTHAZAR
What if conceit have laid my heart to gage?   85
BEL-IMPERIA
Pay that you borrowed and recover it.

71 *disdain* indignation (*O.E.D.*, sb. 2)
74 *oppress* overwhelm with numbers (*O.E.D.*, 1b)
82 *conceit* fancy, imagination
83 *enthralled* enslaved
84 *enlarge* set free
85 *laid . . . to gage* given as a pledge, placed in pawn

77–89 This stichomythia or line-by-line dialogue is a dramatic convention
   deriving from Seneca. For a reference to Kyd's impressive use of the
   convention see Introduction, p. xxix.

BALTHAZAR
  I die if it return from whence it lies.
BEL-IMPERIA
  A heartless man, and live? A miracle!
BALTHAZAR
  Ay lady, love can work such miracles.
LORENZO
  Tush, tush, my lord, let go these ambages,   90
  And in plain terms acquaint her with your love.
BEL-IMPERIA
  What boots complaint, when there's no remedy?
BALTHAZAR
  Yes, to your gracious self must I complain,
  In whose fair answer lies my remedy,
  On whose perfection all my thoughts attend,   95
  On whose aspect mine eyes find beauty's bower,
  In whose translucent breast my heart is lodged.
BEL-IMPERIA
  Alas, my lord, these are but words of course,
  And but device to drive me from this place.
She, in going in, lets fall her glove, which HORATIO, *coming out,*
                                                takes up
HORATIO
  Madam, your glove.   100
BEL-IMPERIA
  Thanks good Horatio, take it for thy pains.
BALTHAZAR
  Signior Horatio stooped in happy time.
HORATIO
  I reaped more grace than I deserved or hoped.
LORENZO
  My Lord, be not dismayed for what is passed,

---

90 *ambages* oblique, roundabout ways of speaking
92 *What boots complaint* What point is there in pleading your love?
96 *aspect* form, appearance
98 *words of course* conventional phrases
99 *device* ed. (deuise *1592*)

---

99 s.d. This rather awkward piece of stage-action may be intended to
  underline the part accident plays in the linked process of 'revenge'.
  Compare the direction 'a letter falleth' (III, ii, 23) and the letter written
  by Pedringano which finds its way by chance into Hieronimo's hands at
  III, vii, 19 ff.

You know that women oft are humorous: 105
These clouds will overblow with little wind;
Let me alone, I'll scatter them myself.
Meanwhile let us devise to spend the time
In some delightful sports and revelling.

HORATIO
The king, my lords, is coming hither straight,   110
To feast the Portingale ambassador:
Things were in readiness before I came.

BALTHAZAR
Then here it fits us to attend the king,
To welcome hither our ambassador,
And learn my father and my country's health.   115

Enter the Banquet, Trumpets, *the* KING, *and* AMBASSADOR

KING
See Lord Ambassador, how Spain entreats
Their prisoner Balthazar, thy viceroy's son:
We pleasure more in kindness than in wars.

AMBASSADOR
Sad is our king, and Portingale laments,
Supposing that Don Balthazar is slain.   120

BALTHAZAR
[*Aside*] So am I slain by beauty's tyranny.
[*To him*] You see, my lord, how Balthazar is slain:
I frolic with the Duke of Castile's son,
Wrapped every hour in pleasures of the court,
And graced with favours of his majesty.   125

KING
Put off your greetings till our feast be done;
Now come and sit with us and taste our cheer.
                              [*They*] *sit to the banquet*
Sit down young prince, you are our second guest;
Brother sit down and nephew take your place;

105 *humorous* temperamental
113 *fits* befits
118 *pleasure* take pleasure

___

115 s.d. *the Banquet, Trumpets* another opportunity for display, underlining
    the proud, self-confident society of the Spanish court. A full-scale
    occasion is evidently intended (not just a buffet-type banquet often
    used on the Elizabethan stage) for they 'sit to the banquet' (l.127 s.d.)
    and remain seated to watch Hieronimo's entertainment.
121 This aside hints the trouble that is breeding under the surface appear-
    ance of order.

Signior Horatio, wait thou upon our cup,   130
For well thou hast deservéd to be honoured.
Now, lordings, fall to; Spain is Portugal,
And Portugal is Spain, we both are friends,
Tribute is paid, and we enjoy our right.
But where is old Hieronimo, our marshal?   135
He promised us, in honour of our guest,
To grace our banquet with some pompous jest.

Enter HIERONIMO *with a* Drum, *three* KNIGHTS, *each* [*with*] *his
scutcheon: then he fetches three* KINGS, [*the* KNIGHTS] *take their
crowns and them captive*

Hieronimo, this masque contents mine eye,
Although I sound not well the mystery.
HIERONIMO
The first armed knight, that hung his scutcheon up,   140
     He takes the scutcheon and gives it to the KING
Was English Robert, Earl of Gloucester,
Who when King Stephen bore sway in Albion,
Arrived with five and twenty thousand men
In Portingale, and by success of war
Enforced the king, then but a Saracen,   145
To bear the yoke of the English monarchy.
KING
My lord of Portingale, by this you see
That which may comfort both your king and you,
And make your late discomfort seem the less.
But say, Hieronimo, what was the next?   150
HIERONIMO
The second knight, that hung his scutcheon up,
                         He doth as he did before

137 *pompous jest* stately entertainment
137 s.d. *Drum* a drummer
137 s.d. *scutcheon* shield with armorial bearings
139 *sound* understand, fathom
139 *mystery* significance, hidden meaning
142 *Albion* England

135 ff. Hieronimo's entertainment appeals to English patriotism at a moment
    (the 1580s or very early 90s) when Spain was the arch-enemy; theatre-
    goers would have expected some patriotic flourish. The history is
    popular rather than academic; for a full discussion of Kyd's sources
    and of his errors concerning the earls of Gloucester and Kent and the
    duke of Lancaster see Boas, pp. 397–8, Edwards, p. 26 fn. and Freeman,
    pp. 55 ff.

Was Edmund, Earl of Kent in Albion,
When English Richard wore the diadem;
He came likewise, and razed Lisbon walls,
And took the King of Portingale in fight: 155
For which, and other suchlike service done,
He after was created Duke of York.

KING

This is another special argument,
That Portingale may deign to bear our yoke,
When it by little England hath been yoked.   160
But now Hieronimo, what were the last?

HIERONIMO

The third and last, not least in our account,
                                        Doing as before

Was as the rest a valiant Englishman,
Brave John of Gaunt, the Duke of Lancaster,
As by his scutcheon plainly may appear.   165
He with a puissant army came to Spain,
And took our King of Castile prisoner.

AMBASSADOR

This is an argument for our viceroy,
That Spain may not insult for her success,
Since English warriors likewise conquered Spain,   170
And made them bow their knees to Albion.

KING

Hieronimo, I drink to thee for this device,
Which hath pleased both the ambassador and me;
Pledge me Hieronimo, if thou love the king.
                                Takes the cup of HORATIO
My lord, I fear we sit but over-long,   175
Unless our dainties were more delicate:
But welcome are you to the best we have.
Now let us in, that you may be despatched,
I think our council is already set.
                                        Exeunt omnes

158 *special* particular, appropriate (*O.E.D.*, 5)
158 *argument* illustration, proof
166 *puissant* powerful   169 *insult* boast
172 *device* show, masque (see l.138)
174 s.d. *of* from
176 *Unless . . . delicate* 'unless it was the case that our food was more
       attractive'

3

Act I, Scene v

ANDREA

Come we for this from depth of underground,
To see him feast that gave me my death's wound?
These pleasant sights are sorrow to my soul,
Nothing but league, and love, and banqueting!

REVENGE

Be still Andrea, ere we go from hence,   5
I'll turn their friendship into fell despite,
Their love to mortal hate, their day to night,
Their hope into despair, their peace to war,
Their joys to pain, their bliss to misery.

Act II, Scene i

Enter LORENZO and BALTHAZAR

LORENZO

My lord, though Bel-imperia seem thus coy,
Let reason hold you in your wonted joy:
'In time the savage bull sustains the yoke,
In time all haggard hawks will stoop to lure,
In time small wedges cleave the hardest oak,   5
In time the flint is pierced with softest shower'—
And she in time will fall from her disdain,
And rue the sufferance of your friendly pain.

6 *fell despite* cruel hatred
1 *coy* disdainful, unresponsive
3 *sustains* undergoes, has to submit to (*O.E.D.*, 9)
4 *haggard* wild, untrained
4 *stoop to lure* swoop down to the lure, a dead bird,or feathers made
    to resemble a bird, used for training hawks
5 *wedges* wedge-shaped pieces of metal used in felling trees
8 *rue* pity   8 *sufferance* patient endurance

---

1 ff. The Andrea—Revenge exchange serves to maintain the audience's
  sense of irony: Revenge plays up (ll.6 ff.) the antitheses of love and
  hate, hope and despair, bliss and misery that underlie it.
3–6 Lorenzo argues in the sonneteering vein extremely popular at this
  date, actually quoting, almost word for word, a sonnet in Thomas
  Watson's *Hecatompathia* (entered for publication 1582). The lines
  represent conventional notions about the courtship of reluctant ladies,
  and therefore deliberately adopt the artifices of up-to-date poetry on
  the subject. Line 3 is recalled in *Much Ado* (I, i, 258) as Don Pedro
  prophesies that even Benedick will fall victim to love.

BALTHAZAR
'No, she is wilder, and more hard withal,
Than beast, or bird, or tree, or stony wall'.   10
But wherefore blot I Bel-imperia's name?
It is my fault, not she, that merits blame.
My feature is not to content her sight,
My words are rude and work her no delight.
The lines I send her are but harsh and ill,   15
Such as do drop from Pan and Marsyas' quill.
My presents are not of sufficient cost,
And being worthless all my labour's lost.
Yet might she love me for my valiancy;
Ay, but that's slandered by captivity.   20
Yet might she love me to content her sire;
Ay, but her reason masters his desire.
Yet might she love me as her brother's friend;
Ay, but her hopes aim at some other end.
Yet might she love me to uprear her state;   25
Ay, but perhaps she hopes some nobler mate.
Yet might she love me as her beauty's thrall;
Ay, but I fear she cannot love at all.

13 *feature* form, bearing (not merely the face)
13 *to* such as to
16 *Pan and Marsyas* each of these gods, in different stories, challen-
    ged Apollo to contests in flute-playing; neither could match his
    skill and both were punished
16 *quill* either a musical pipe or a pen; Kyd appears to use both
    senses here
19 *valiancy* valour
20 *slandered* brought into disrepute (*O.E.D.*, v, 2)
25 *uprear her state* improve her social position
27 *beauty's* ed. (beauteous *1592*)

9–10 Balthazar quotes (with variation) the lines of Watson's sonnet that
    follow those quoted by Lorenzo. (The original reads: 'More fierce
    is my sweet loue, more hard withall, / Then Beast, or Birde, then Tree,
    or Stony wall.') The two young men are showing their familiarity with
    contemporary poetry.
11–28 Balthazar's speech became famous, and was often parodied. The
    parodists, like modern readers, are no doubt reacting against this
    highly artificial and self-conscious way of dramatising indecision and
    self-doubt. Balthazar must of course be at least half-ridiculous here,
    being excessively in love, and being in any case a weak nature.

LORENZO
    My lord, for my sake leave these ecstasies,
    And doubt not but we'll find some remedy.   30
    Some cause there is that lets you not be loved:
    First that must needs be known, and then removed.
    What if my sister love some other knight?
BALTHAZAR
    My summer's day will turn to winter's night.
LORENZO
    I have already found a stratagem,   35
    To sound the bottom of this doubtful theme.
    My lord, for once you shall be ruled by me:
    Hinder me not whate'er you hear or see.
    By force or fair means will I cast about
    To find the truth of all this question out.   40
    Ho, Pedringano!
PEDRINGANO   [*Within*] Signior!
LORENZO   *Vien qui presto.*

Enter PEDRINGANO

PEDRINGANO
    Hath your lordship any service to command me?
LORENZO
    Ay, Pedringano, service of import.
    And not to spend the time in trifling words,
    Thus stands the case: it is not long thou know'st,   45
    Since I did shield thee from my father's wrath,
    For thy conveyance in Andrea's love,
    For which thou wert adjudged to punishment.
    I stood betwixt thee and thy punishment;
    And since, thou know'st how I have favoured thee.   50
    Now to these favours will I add reward,
    Not with fair words, but store of golden coin,
    And lands and living joined with dignities,

---

29 *ecstasies* unreasoning passions (Edwards)
36 *sound the bottom* discover the exact features (the metaphor is
    from 'sounding' a waterway to detect snags and shallows)
41 *Vien qui presto* Come here quickly (Italian)
41 *qui* ed. (*que 1592*)
47 *conveyance* secret or underhand dealing
52 *store* abundance

---

29 *ecstasies* Lorenzo's word shows that Kyd meant Balthazar's speech
    to be delivered in an exaggerated fashion.

If thou but satisfy my just demand.
Tell truth and have me for thy lasting friend.　　　　55
PEDRINGANO
Whate'er it be your lordship shall demand,
My bounden duty bids me tell the truth,
If case it lie in me to tell the truth.
LORENZO
Then, Pedringano, this is my demand:
Whom loves my sister Bel-imperia?　　　　60
For she reposeth all her trust in thee—
Speak man, and gain both friendship and reward:
I mean, whom loves she in Andrea's place?
PEDRINGANO
Alas, my lord, since Don Andrea's death,
I have no credit with her as before,　　　　65
And therefore know not if she love or no.
LORENZO
Nay, if thou dally then I am thy foe,　　　*[Draws his sword]*
And fear shall force what friendship cannot win.
Thy death shall bury what thy life conceals.
Thou diest for more esteeming her than me.　　　　70
PEDRINGANO
O, stay, my lord.
LORENZO
Yet speak the truth and I will guerdon thee,
And shield thee from whatever can ensue,
And will conceal whate'er proceeds from thee:
But if thou dally once again, thou diest.　　　　75
PEDRINGANO
If Madam Bel-imperia be in love—
LORENZO
What, villain, ifs and ands?
　　　　　　　　　　　　　　　[Offers to kill him]
PEDRINGANO
O stay my lord, she loves Horatio.
　　　　　　　　　　　BALTHAZAR *starts back*

58 *it lie in me* I am able to
71 *stay* wait, hold off
72 *guerdon* reward

---

77 *ifs and ands* 'ifs and ifs' (and used to mean 'if'). A strong theatrical
moment (as Lorenzo lunges at Pedringano) that Nashe may be remembering in his preface to Greene's *Menaphon*, where he writes of
'translators' who are content 'to bodge up a blank verse with ifs and
ands'.

LORENZO
  What, Don Horatio our Knight Marshal's son?
PEDRINGANO
  Even him my lord.   80
LORENZO
  Now say but how know'st thou he is her love,
  And thou shalt find me kind and liberal:
  Stand up, I say, and fearless tell the truth.
PEDRINGANO
  She sent him letters which myself perused,
  Full-fraught with lines and arguments of love,   85
  Preferring him before Prince Balthazar.
LORENZO
  Swear on this cross that what thou say'st is true,
  And that thou wilt conceal what thou hast told.
PEDRINGANO
  I swear to both by him that made us all.
LORENZO
  In hope thine oath is true, here's thy reward,   90
  But if I prove thee perjured and unjust,
  This very sword whereon thou took'st thine oath,
  Shall be the worker of thy tragedy.
PEDRINGANO
  What I have said is true, and shall for me
  Be still concealed from Bel-imperia.   95
  Besides, your honour's liberality
  Deserves my duteous service even till death.
LORENZO
  Let this be all that thou shalt do for me:
  Be watchful when, and where, these lovers meet,
  And give me notice in some secret sort.   100
PEDRINGANO
  I will my lord.
LORENZO
  Then shalt thou find that I am liberal.
  Thou know'st that I can more advance thy state
  Than she, be therefore wise and fail me not.
  Go and attend her as thy custom is,   105

85 *fraught* loaded
87 *this cross* his sword-hilt
90 *In hope* in the faith that
91 *unjust* false, dishonest   100 *in sort* by some secret means
103 *advance thy state* improve your social position and your finances

Lest absence make her think thou dost amiss.

Exit PEDRINGANO

Why so: *tam armis quam ingenio:*
Where words prevail not, violence prevails;
But gold doth more than either of them both.
How likes Prince Balthazar this stratagem?   110

BALTHAZAR

Both well, and ill: it makes me glad and sad:
Glad, that I know the hinderer of my love,
Sad, that I fear she hates me whom I love.
Glad, that I know on whom to be revenged,
Sad, that she'll fly me if I take revenge.   115
Yet must I take revenge or die myself,
For love resisted grows impatient.
I think Horatio be my destined plague:
First, in his hand he brandished a sword,
And with that sword he fiercely waged war,   120
And in that war he gave me dangerous wounds,
And by those wounds he forced me to yield,
And by my yielding I became his slave.
Now in his mouth he carries pleasing words,
Which pleasing words do harbour sweet conceits,   125
Which sweet conceits are limed with sly deceits,
Which sly deceits smooth Bel-imperia's ears,
And through her ears dive down into her heart,
And in her heart set him where I should stand.
Thus hath he ta'en my body by his force,   130
And now by sleight would captivate my soul:
But in his fall I'll tempt the destinies,
And either lose my life, or win my love.

107 *tam . . . ingenio* by equal parts of force and skill
125 *sweet conceits* pleasing figures of speech
126 *limed with* made into traps with (from bird-lime, a gluey sub-
     stance used to catch birds)
127 *smooth* seduce, flatter (compare *O.E.D.*, v, 5a)
131 *sleight* trickery
132 *in his fall* in causing his downfall

111–33 Clemen (pp. 106–7) usefully comments: 'the lack of substance in
     this repetitive style of his, tediously amplified by antithesis and other
     rhetorical figures, is exactly in keeping with the irresolute, dependent,
     puppet-like role that Balthazar is to sustain in the play.' His speech
     here parallels and complements his lines on Bel-imperia (ll.9 ff.)
     near the scene's beginning.

LORENZO

    Let's go, my lord, your staying stays revenge.
    Do you but follow me and gain your love: 135
    Her favour must be won by his remove.   *Exeunt*

Act II, Scene ii

Enter HORATIO *and* BEL-IMPERIA

HORATIO

    Now, madam, since by favour of your love
    Our hidden smoke is turned to open flame,
    And that with looks and words we feed our thoughts
    (Two chief contents, where more cannot be had),
    Thus in the midst of love's fair blandishments,   5
    Why show you sign of inward languishments?
        PEDRINGANO *showeth all to the* PRINCE *and* LORENZO, *placing*
                them in secret [*above*]

BEL-IMPERIA

    My heart, sweet friend, is like a ship at sea:
    She wisheth port, where riding all at ease,
    She may repair what stormy times have worn,
    And leaning on the shore, may sing with joy   10
    That pleasure follows pain, and bliss annoy.
    Possession of thy love is th'only port,
    Wherein my heart, with fears and hopes long tossed,
    Each hour doth wish and long to make resort;
    There to repair the joys that it hath lost,   15
    And sitting safe, to sing in Cupid's choir
    That sweetest bliss is crown of love's desire.

  3 *thoughts* ed. (though *1592*) wishes, imaginings
  4 *contents* sources of contentment
  7 *friend* love (a common Elizabethan sense)
  9 *may* ed. (mad *1592*)
 15 *repair* restore
 16 *sing* celebrate
 17 *is* which is
 17 *1592* has s.d. '*Balthazar* above'; Edwards suggests, convincingly,
    that this is a note by the author to clarify the earlier direction (l.6)
    and need not be repeated

---

  6 s.d. Balthazar and Lorenzo watch the lovers from the upper-stage or
  balcony. Edwards is, I think, correct in arguing that *1592*'s 'Balthazar
  aboue.' after l.17 is an author's clarification; like him I transfer the
  'above' to the end of the present direction.

BALTHAZAR

   O sleep mine eyes, see not my love profaned;
   Be deaf, my ears, hear not my discontent;
   Die, heart, another joys what thou deservest.   20

LORENZO

   Watch still mine eyes, to see this love disjoined;
   Hear still mine ears, to hear them both lament;
   Live, heart, to joy at fond Horatio's fall.

BEL-IMPERIA

   Why stands Horatio speechless all this while?

HORATIO

   The less I speak, the more I meditate.   25

BEL-IMPERIA

   But whereon dost thou chiefly meditate?

HORATIO

   On dangers past, and pleasures to ensue.

BALTHAZAR

   On pleasures past, and dangers to ensue.

BEL-IMPERIA

   What dangers and what pleasures dost thou mean?

HORATIO

   Dangers of war and pleasures of our love.   30

LORENZO

   Dangers of death, but pleasures none at all.

BEL-IMPERIA

   Let dangers go, thy war shall be with me,
   But such a war as breaks no bond of peace.
   Speak thou fair words, I'll cross them with fair words;
   Send thou sweet looks, I'll meet them with sweet looks;   35
   Write loving lines, I'll answer loving lines;
   Give me a kiss, I'll countercheck thy kiss:
   Be this our warring peace, or peaceful war.

HORATIO

   But gracious madam, then appoint the field
   Where trial of this war shall first be made.   40

20 *joys* enjoys   23 *fond* foolish, besotted
33 *war* ed. (warring *1592*)
34 *cross* meet, complement (a punning reference to cross meaning
   thwart, go counter to, is intended)
37 *countercheck* oppose, take countering action against

18 ff. The antithetical speeches by the lovers and those watching them is
    one of Kyd's more obvious ways of insisting on dramatic irony. Bel-
    imperia's description of the bower (ll.42 ff.) is also obviously and
    grimly ironic.

BALTHAZAR
    Ambitious villain, how his boldness grows!
BEL-IMPERIA
    Then be thy father's pleasant bower the field,
    Where first we vowed a mutual amity:
    The court were dangerous, that place is safe.
    Our hour shall be when Vesper gins to rise,   45
    That summons home distressful travellers.
    There none shall hear us but the harmless birds:
    Happily the gentle nightingale
    Shall carol us asleep ere we be ware,
    And singing with the prickle at her breast,   50
    Tell our delight and mirthful dalliance.
    Till then each hour will seem a year and more.
HORATIO
    But, honey sweet, and honourable love,
    Return we now into your father's sight:
    Dangerous suspicion waits on our delight.   55
LORENZO
    Ay, danger mixed with jealous despite
    Shall send thy soul into eternal night.   *Exeunt*

Act II, Scene iii

Enter KING *of Spain,* Portingale AMBASSADOR, DON CYPRIAN, *etc.*

KING
    Brother of Castile, to the prince's love
    What says your daughter Bel-imperia?
CASTILE
    Although she coy it as becomes her kind,
    And yet dissemble that she loves the prince,
    I doubt not, I, but she will stoop in time.   5

42 *bower* an arbour, or enclosed garden-seat, covered with branches
    of trees, plants etc. Cf. II, iv, 53 s.d. and note
45 *Vesper* the evening star or Venus
46 *distressful travellers* weary labourers ('travel' and 'travail' were
    closely linked in Elizabethan use)
48 *Happily* haply, perhaps
50 *prickle* thorn
56 *jealous* ed. (jealous *1592*) watchful, suspicious; metre requires
    three syllables
 3 *coy it* affects disinclination
 3 *as becomes her kind* as it is a woman's nature to do
 5 *stoop* become obedient; and compare II, i, 4 and note

And were she froward, which she will not be,
Yet herein shall she follow my advice,
Which is to love him or forgo my love.
KING
Then, Lord Ambassador of Portingale,
Advise thy king to make this marriage up,   10
For strengthening of our late-confirmed league;
I know no better means to make us friends.
Her dowry shall be large and liberal:
Besides that she is daughter and half-heir
Unto our brother here, Don Cyprian,   15
And shall enjoy the moiety of his land,
I'll grace her marriage with an uncle's gift.
And this it is: in case the match go forward,
The tribute which you pay shall be released,
And if by Balthazar she have a son,   20
He shall enjoy the kingdom after us.
AMBASSADOR
I'll make the motion to my sovereign liege,
And work it if my counsel may prevail.
KING
Do so, my lord, and if he give consent,
I hope his presence here will honour us   25
In celebration of the nuptial day—
And let himself determine of the time.
AMBASSADOR
Will't please your grace command me aught beside?
KING
Commend me to the king, and so farewell.
But where's Prince Balthazar to take his leave?   30
AMBASSADOR
That is performed already, my good lord.
KING
Amongst the rest of what you have in charge,
The prince's ransom must not be forgot;
That's none of mine, but his that took him prisoner,
And well his forwardness deserves reward: 35
It was Horatio, our Knight Marshal's son.

6 *froward* perverse, refractory
16 *moiety* a half-share
22 *make the motion* put the proposal
35 *forwardness* enterprise, zeal

AMBASSADOR
　　Between us there's a price already pitched,
　　And shall be sent with all convenient speed.
KING
　　Then once again farewell, my lord.
AMBASSADOR
　　Farewell, my Lord of Castile and the rest.   *Exit*   40
KING
　　Now, brother, you must take some little pains
　　To win fair Bel-imperia from her will:
　　Young virgins must be ruled by their friends.
　　The prince is amiable, and loves her well,
　　If she neglect him and forgo his love,   45
　　She both will wrong her own estate and ours.
　　Therefore, whiles I do entertain the prince
　　With greatest pleasure that our court affords,
　　Endeavour you to win your daughter's thought:
　　If she give back, all this will come to naught.   *Exeunt*   50

Act II, Scene iv

Enter HORATIO, BEL-IMPERIA, *and* PEDRINGANO

HORATIO
　　Now that the night begins with sable wings
　　To overcloud the brightness of the sun,
　　And that in darkness pleasures may be done,
　　Come Bel-imperia, let us to the bower,
　　And there in safety pass a pleasant hour.   5
BEL-IMPERIA
　　I follow thee my love, and will not back,
　　Although my fainting heart controls my soul.
HORATIO
　　Why, make you doubt of Pedringano's faith?

37 *pitched* agreed
42 *will* wilfulness
49 *thought* ed. (thoughts *1592*)
50 *give back* 'turn her back on us' (Edwards), refuse
　1 *sable* black
　7 *controls* oppresses, masters (the heart's fearfulness struggles
　　against the soul's wishes)

1–5 An Elizabethan audience would immediately feel the irony of
　　invoking night, associated with evil, to watch over the relationship.
　　The ironies are strengthened in the next lines; see esp. ll.16–19.

BEL-IMPERIA

No, he is as trusty as my second self.
Go Pedringano, watch without the gate,   10
And let us know if any make approach.

PEDRINGANO

[*Aside*] Instead of watching, I'll deserve more gold
By fetching Don Lorenzo to this match.

Exit PEDRINGANO

HORATIO

What means my love?

BEL-IMPERIA   I know not what myself.
And yet my heart foretells me some mischance.   15

HORATIO

Sweet say not so, fair fortune is our friend,
And heavens have shut up day to pleasure us.
The stars thou see'st hold back their twinkling shine,
And Luna hides herself to pleasure us.

BEL-IMPERIA

Thou hast prevailed, I'll conquer my misdoubt,   20
And in thy love and counsel drown my fear.
I fear no more, love now is all my thoughts.
Why sit we not? for pleasure asketh ease.

HORATIO

The more thou sit'st within these leafy bowers,
The more will Flora deck it with her flowers.   25

BEL-IMPERIA

Ay, but if Flora spy Horatio here,
Her jealous eye will think I sit too near.

HORATIO

Hark, madam, how the birds record by night,
For joy that Bel-imperia sits in sight.

BEL-IMPERIA

No, Cupid counterfeits the nightingale,   30
To frame sweet music to Horatio's tale.

HORATIO

If Cupid sing, then Venus is not far:
Ay, thou art Venus or some fairer star.

---

10 *without* outside   13 *match* meeting
19 *Luna* the moon   23 *asketh* needs, requires
28 *record* sing
31 *frame* adapt, compose

32-5 *Venus . . . Mars* Aphrodite (Venus) was unfaithful to her husband
Hephaestus with Ares (Mars) the god of war.

BEL-IMPERIA
If I be Venus, thou must needs be Mars,
And where Mars reigneth, there must needs be wars.   35
HORATIO
Then thus begin our wars: put forth thy hand,
That it may combat with my ruder hand.
BEL-IMPERIA
Set forth thy foot to try the push of mine.
HORATIO
But first my looks shall combat against thine.
BEL-IMPERIA
Then ward thyself: I dart this kiss at thee.   40
HORATIO
Thus I retort the dart thou threw'st at me.
BEL-IMPERIA
Nay then, to gain the glory of the field,
My twining arms shall yoke and make thee yield.
HORATIO
Nay then, my arms are large and strong withal:
Thus elms by vines are compassed till they fall.   45
BEL-IMPERIA
O let me go, for in my troubled eyes
Now may'st thou read that life in passion dies.
HORATIO
O stay a while and I will die with thee,
So shalt thou yield and yet have conquered me.
BEL-IMPERIA
Who's there? Pedringano! We are betrayed!   50

35 *wars* ed. (war *1592*); rhyme requires the plural form
37 *ruder* rougher, coarser
40 *ward* guard, shield
44 *withal* ed. (with *1592*)
50 *Who's there? Pedringano!* ed. (Whose there *Pedringano? 1592*)

43–5 Edwards shows that Horatio here inverts a familiar saying about the elm (usually an emblem of friendship: the vine holds up the tree in its embraces); taken with the double meaning in 'die' (a common sexual pun), it becomes obvious that Kyd wishes to emphasise the sensuality of the moment, thus making the ironies more emotionally charged. The literal sense of 1.48 does of course come about; a somewhat heavy-handed irony.

Enter LORENZO, BALTHAZAR, SERBERINE, PEDRINGANO, *disguised*

LORENZO
My lord, away with her, take her aside.
O sir, forbear, your valour is already tried.
Quickly despatch, my masters.

They hang him in the arbour

HORATIO
What, will you murder me?

LORENZO
Ay, thus, and thus; these are the fruits of love.   55

They stab him

BEL-IMPERIA
O save his life and let me die for him!
O save him, brother, save him, Balthazar:
I loved Horatio, but he loved not me.

BALTHAZAR
But Balthazar loves Bel-imperia.

LORENZO
Although his life were still ambitious proud,   60
Yet is he at the highest now he is dead.

BEL-IMPERIA
Murder! murder! Help, Hieronimo, help!

LORENZO
Come, stop her mouth, away with her.

Exeunt, [leaving HORATIO'S *body]*

---

52 *tried* tested, proved. The thought of Horatio's martial prowess
   still rankles with Lorenzo
60 *ambitious proud* ambitious for a position that would satisfy his
   pride

---

53 s.d. Whether a stage-tree was used for this purpose remains unclear;
   Isabella (IV, ii, 6 ff.) seems to refer to a tree; Hieronimo says (IV, iv,
   111) he found Horatio 'hanging on a tree'; the author of the Fourth
   Addition thinks very specifically of a tree (see ll.60 ff.). But editors
   may well be right in arguing that the arbour illustrated on the title-page
   of the 1615 edition (a trellis-work arch with a seat in it) may have been
   decorated with leaves and branches, and so have served as both arbour
   and tree.

Act II, Scene v

Enter HIERONIMO *in his shirt, etc.*

HIERONIMO
What outcries pluck me from my naked bed,
And chill my throbbing heart with trembling fear,
Which never danger yet could daunt before?
Who calls Hieronimo? Speak, here I am.
I did not slumber, therefore 'twas no dream,   5
No, no, it was some woman cried for help,
And here within this garden did she cry,
And in this garden must I rescue her.
But stay, what murderous spectacle is this?
A man hanged up and all the murderers gone,   10
And in my bower to lay the guilt on me.
This place was made for pleasure not for death.

                              He cuts him down

Those garments that he wears I oft have seen—
Alas, it is Horatio, my sweet son!
Oh no, but he that whilom was my son.   15
O was it thou that calledst me from my bed?
O speak, if any spark of life remain:
I am thy father. Who hath slain my son?
What savage monster, not of human kind,
Hath here been glutted with thy harmless blood,   20
And left thy bloody corpse dishonoured here,
For me, amidst this dark and deathful shades,
To drown thee with an ocean of my tears?

1 s.d. *shirt* nightshirt
1 *naked bed* a transferred epithet; the sleeper is naked (or lightly clothed).
  Edwards says the phrase was familiar
15 *whilom* in the past, till now
22 *this* an accepted plural form at this date

1 s.d. For a description of probable stage-practice here see Fourth
  Addition ll.135–9.
1–33 Hieronimo's soliloquy, perhaps the most famous of the play,
  is one which, as Clemen (p. 103) points out, 'is not only spoken but
  acted', carrying its own internal 'stage-directions', a technique followed,
  and made more subtle, by Shakespeare.
12 continuing the pleasure / death irony of II, ii and II, iv.
13 ff. Good direction and acting can make the moment of discovery
  deeply poignant. Kyd's words may seem absurdly simple here, but he is
  surely right not to overload Hieronimo's speech with rhetoric.

O heavens, why made you night to cover sin?
By day this deed of darkness had not been.   25
O earth, why didst thou not in time devour
The vild profaner of this sacred bower?
O poor Horatio, what hadst thou misdone,
To leese thy life ere life was new begun?
O wicked butcher, whatsoe'er thou wert,   30
How could thou strangle virtue and desert?
Ay me most wretched, that have lost my joy,
In leesing my Horatio, my sweet boy!

Enter ISABELLA

ISABELLA
My husband's absence makes my heart to throb—
Hieronimo!   35
HIERONIMO
Here, Isabella, help me to lament,
For sighs are stopped and all my tears are spent.
ISABELLA
What world of grief! My son Horatio!
O where's the author of this endless woe?
HIERONIMO
To know the author were some ease of grief,   40
For in revenge my heart would find relief.
ISABELLA
Then is he gone? and is my son gone too?
O, gush out, tears, fountains and floods of tears;
Blow, sighs, and raise an everlasting storm:
For outrage fits our cursed wretchedness.   45
HIERONIMO
Sweet lovely rose, ill plucked before thy time,
Fair worthy son, not conquered, but betrayed:
I'll kiss thee now, for words with tears are stayed.
ISABELLA
And I'll close up the glasses of his sight,
For once these eyes were only my delight.   50

26 *in time* at the due moment
27 *vild* vile   29 *leese* lose
29 *was new begun* had entered a new phase; perhaps the reference is
   to Horatio's new life as a prominent citizen after his success in
   war   39 *author* the one responsible
45 *outrage* passionate behaviour (*O.E.D.*, sb. 2)   48 *with* by
48 *stayed* ed. (stainde *1592*) stopped
49 *glasses of his sight* his eyes

HIERONIMO

See'st thou this handkercher besmeared with blood?
It shall not from me till I take revenge.
See'st thou those wounds that yet are bleeding fresh?
I'll not entomb them till I have revenged.
Then will I joy amidst my discontent, 55
Till then my sorrow never shall be spent.

ISABELLA

The heavens are just, murder cannot be hid:
Time is the author both of truth and right,
And time will bring this treachery to light.

HIERONIMO

Meanwhile, good Isabella, cease thy plaints, 60
Or at the least dissemble them awhile:
So shall we sooner find the practice out,
And learn by whom all this was brought about.
Come Isabel, now let us take him up,

They take him up

And bear him in from out this cursed place. 65
I'll say his dirge, singing fits not this case.
O aliquis mihi quas pulchrum ver educat herbas

51 *handkercher* hankderchief, small scarf
60 *plaints* complaints, sorrowing   62 *practice* plot
66 *dirge* funeral song or hymn (from *dirige*, the first word of a Latin
antiphon in the office for the dead)
67 *ver educat* ed. (*var educet 1592*)

51–2 For the possible origin of this 'handkercher' see I, iv, 42 note.
57–9 Isabella's words are a common Elizabethan axiom (see Tilley M1315),
skilfully used by Kyd to contrast with Hieronimo's complete bewilderment.
67–80 'Let someone bind for me the herbs which beautiful spring fosters,
and let a salve be given for our grief; or let him apply juices, if there are
any that bring forgetfulness to men's minds. I myself shall gather
anywhere in the great world whatever plants the sun draws forth into
the fair regions of light; I myself shall drink whatever drug the wise-
woman devises, and whatever herbs incantation assembles by its
secret power. I shall face all things, death even, until the moment our
every feeling dies in this dead breast. And so shall I never again, my
life, see those eyes of yours, and has everlasting slumber sealed up your
light of life? I shall perish with you; thus, thus would it please me to go
to the shades below. But none the less I shall keep myself from yielding
to a hastened death, lest in that case no revenge should follow your death'.
The passage, which contains reminiscences of Lucretius, Vergil and
Ovid, is 'a *pastiche*, in Kyd's singular fashion, of tags from classical
poetry, and lines of his own composition' (Boas).

HIERONIMO *sets his breast unto his sword*
Misceat, et nostro detur medicina dolori;
Aut, si qui faciunt animis oblivia, succos
Praebeat; ipse metam magnum quaecunque per orbem   70
Gramina Sol pulchras effert in luminis oras;
Ipse bibam quicquid meditatur saga veneni,
Quicquid et herbarum vi caeca nenia nectit:
Omnia perpetiar, lethum quoque, dum semel omnis
Noster in extincto moriatur pectore sensus.   75
Ergo tuos oculos nunquam, mea vita, videbo,
Et tua perpetuus sepelivit lumina somnus?
Emoriar tecum: sic, sic juvat ire sub umbras.
At tamen absistam properato cedere letho,
Ne mortem vindicta tuam tum nulla sequatur.   80
Here he throws it from him and bears the body away

Act II, Scene vi

ANDREA
Brought'st thou me hither to increase my pain?
I looked that Balthazar should have been slain;
But 'tis my friend Horatio that is slain,
And they abuse fair Bel-imperia,
On whom I doted more than all the world,   5
Because she loved me more than all the world.
REVENGE
Thou talk'st of harvest when the corn is green:
The end is crown of every work well done;
The sickle comes not till the corn be ripe.
Be still, and ere I lead thee from this place,   10
I'll show thee Balthazar in heavy case.

69 *animis oblivia* ed. (*annum oblimia 1592*)
70 *metam magnum quaecunque* ed. (*metum magnam quicunque 1592*)
71 *effert* ed. (*effecit 1592*)
72 *veneni* ed. (*veneri 1592*)
73 *herbarum vi caeca nenia* ed. (*irraui euecaeca menia 1592*)
75 *pectore* ed. (*pectora 1592*)
80 *tum* ed. (*tam 1592*)
 2 *looked* expected, hoped
 5 *On* ed. (Or *1592*)
11 *in heavy case* in a sad state

---

1 ff. One effect of the Andrea–Revenge exchange is to maintain an
   audience's detachment, threatened by the emotion-laden events of the
   past scenes.

Act III, Scene i

Enter VICEROY *of Portingale,* NOBLES, VILLUPPO

VICEROY
　Infortunate condition of kings,
　Seated amidst so many helpless doubts!
　First we are placed upon extremest height,
　And oft supplanted with exceeding heat,
　But ever subject to the wheel of chance;　　　　5
　And at our highest never joy we so,
　As we both doubt and dread our overthrow.
　So striveth not the waves with sundry winds
　As Fortune toileth in the affairs of kings,
　That would be feared, yet fear to be beloved,　　10
　Sith fear or love to kings is flattery.
　For instance, lordings, look upon your king,
　By hate deprived of his dearest son,
　The only hope of our successive line.
1 NOBLEMAN
　I had not thought that Alexandro's heart　　　　15
　Had been envenomed with such extreme hate:
　But now I see that words have several works,
　And there's no credit in the countenance.

---

1 s.d. NOBLES, VILLUPPO ed. (*Nobles, Alexandro, Villuppo 1592*)
1 *Infortunate* ill-used by Fortune
2 *Seated* placed
2 *helpless* for which there is no help
2 *doubts* fears　　　4 *heat* fury
10 *would be* wish to be　　　11 *Sith* since
12 *lordings* lords
14 *successive line* line of succession
15 s.p 1 NOBLEMAN ed. (*Nob. 1592*)
17 *words have several works* i.e. what a man does may not always
　reflect what he says
18 *no credit in* no point in trusting

1–11 A common theme in Elizabethan writing (see e.g. *Richard II*,
　III, ii, 155 ff.) and with parallels also in Seneca (see *Agamemnon*,
　57–73).
5 *the wheel of chance* the common Elizabethan figure to describe the
　cycle of achievement and failure in human (and especially political)
　life: kings rise to the top of the wheel in prosperity and fall, inevitably,
　to its lowest point in defeat and death. See Introduction, p. xxiv for
　the ironies of this speech and this scene.

VILLUPPO
  No, for, my lord, had you beheld the train
  That feigned love had coloured in his looks,   20
  When he in camp consorted Balthazar,
  Far more inconstant had you thought the sun,
  That hourly coasts the centre of the earth,
  Than Alexandro's purpose to the prince.
VICEROY
  No more, Villuppo, thou hast said enough,   25
  And with thy words thou slay'st our wounded thoughts.
  Nor shall I longer dally with the world,
  Procrastinating Alexandro's death:
  Go some of you and fetch the traitor forth,
  That as he is condemned he may die.   30

    Enter ALEXANDRO *with a* NOBLEMAN *and* HALBERTS

2 NOBLEMAN
  In such extremes will naught but patience serve.
ALEXANDRO
  But in extremes what patience shall I use?
  Nor discontents it me to leave the world,
  With whom there nothing can prevail but wrong.
2 NOBLEMAN
  Yet hope the best.
ALEXANDRO   'Tis Heaven is my hope.   35

21 *consorted* associated with, kept company with
24 *purpose* attitude, relationship
30 s.d. HALBERTS halberdiers; see I, iv, 21 note
31 s.p. 2 NOBLEMAN ed. (*Nob. 1592*)
34 *With . . . wrong* i.e. Since all I ever meet is injustice

19–20 'if you had seen the false appearance [of friendship] that pretended
    love had counterfeited in his face.' 'Train' literally means 'treachery';
    Villuppo uses the word to describe the false appearance of love (a
    treacherous mask) Alexandro is accused of wearing.
23 *That hourly . . . earth* 'that with a regular motion (in a precise number
    of hours) circles this earth, the centre of the universe.' Kyd writes
    in terms of the old cosmology; the sun's (apparent) circling often
    served as a metaphor for constancy.
32–7 Alexandro's sense of life's injustices anticipates much that Hieronimo
    has to say in the next scene: part of the 'overlapping' technique Kyd
    uses so successfully (see III, ii, 3 ff.).

As for the earth, it is too much infect
To yield me hope of any of her mould.

VICEROY

Why linger ye? bring forth that daring fiend,
And let him die for his accursed deed.

ALEXANDRO

Not that I fear the extremity of death,   40
For nobles cannot stoop to servile fear,
Do I, O king, thus discontented live.
But this, O this, torments my labouring soul,
That thus I die suspected of a sin,
Whereof, as heavens have known my secret thoughts,   45
So am I free from this suggestion.

VICEROY

No more, I say! to the tortures! when!
Bind him, and burn his body in those flames,
                              They bind him to the stake
That shall prefigure those unquenched fires
Of Phlegethon prepared for his soul.   50

ALEXANDRO

My guiltless death will be avenged on thee,
On thee, Villuppo, that hath maliced thus,
Or for thy meed hast falsely me accused.

VILLUPPO

Nay, Alexandro, if thou menace me,
I'll lend a hand to send thee to the lake   55
Where those thy words shall perish with thy works—
Injurious traitor, monstrous homicide!

Enter AMBASSADOR

AMBASSADOR

Stay, hold a while,
And here, with pardon of his majesty,
Lay hands upon Villuppo.

36 *infect* infected
37 *To yield . . . mould* i.e. to allow me to place any faith in anyone
   born and brought up there
46 *suggestion* false accusation (*O.E.D.*, 3)
47 *when!* an impatient exclamation
50 *Phlegethon* the mythical river of hell whose waves were of fire
52 *maliced* entertained malice (*O.E.D.*, v, 2)
53 *meed* reward, advantage
55 *lake* the lake of Acheron in hell, into which Phlegethon (l.50)
   flows

VICEROY   Ambassador,   60
What news hath urged this sudden entrance?
AMBASSADOR
Know, sovereign lord, that Balthazar doth live.
VICEROY
What say'st thou? liveth Balthazar our son?
AMBASSADOR
Your highness' son, Lord Balthazar, doth live;
And, well entreated in the court of Spain,   65
Humbly commends him to your majesty.
These eyes beheld, and these my followers;
With these, the letters of the king's commends,
                              Gives him letters
Are happy witnesses of his highness' health.
                    The VICEROY *looks on the letters, and proceeds*
VICEROY
[*Reads*] 'Thy son doth live, your tribute is received,   70
Thy peace is made, and we are satisfied.
The rest resolve upon as things proposed
For both our honours and thy benefit.'
AMBASSADOR
These are his highness' farther articles.
                              He gives him more letters
VICEROY
Accursed wretch, to intimate these ills   75
Against the life and reputation
Of noble Alexandro! Come, my lord,
Let him unbind thee that is bound to death,
To make a quital for thy discontent.
                              They unbind him

58–61 lineation ed. (Stay . . . Maiestie,/Lay . . . *Villuppo.*/Embassa-
    dour . . . entrance? *1592*)
61 *entrance* three syllables   68 *commends* greetings
69 s.d. VICEROY ed. (*King 1592*)
72 *resolve upon* decide upon 75 *intimate* make known, announce publicly
77 *Come, my lord,* ed. (come my lord vnbinde him. *1592*)
79 *quital* requital, recompense

77 *Come, my lord 1592* adds 'vnbinde him', but this gives the line thirteen
    syllables. The extra words may have been included into the text from a
    stage-direction placed too early (and not cancelled when the direction
    at l.79 was added), or they may result from a compositor's anticipation
    of that direction. Edwards must be right to omit them.
79 s.d. Villuppo unbinds Alexandro as the text directs; 'they unbind him'
    is used to mean 'he is unbound'.

ALEXANDRO
    Dread lord, in kindness you could do no less,   80
    Upon report of such a damned fact.
    But thus we see our innocence hath saved
    The hopeless life which thou, Villuppo, sought
    By thy suggestions to have massacred.
VICEROY
    Say, false Villuppo, wherefore didst thou thus   85
    Falsely betray Lord Alexandro's life?
    Him, whom thou knowest that no unkindness else,
    But even the slaughter of our dearest son,
    Could once have moved us to have misconceived.
ALEXANDRO
    Say, treacherous Villuppo, tell the king,   90
    Wherein hath Alexandro used thee ill?
VILLUPPO
    Rent with remembrance of so foul a deed,
    My guilty soul submits me to thy doom:
    For not for Alexandro's injuries,
    But for reward and hope to be preferred,   95
    Thus have I shamelessly hazarded his life.
VICEROY
    Which, villain, shall be ransomed with thy death,
    And not so mean a torment as we here
    Devised for him who thou said'st slew our son,
    But with the bitterest torments and extremes   100
    That may be yet invented for thine end.
                  ALEXANDRO *seems to entreat*
    Entreat me not, go, take the traitor hence.
                   Exit VILLUPPO [*guarded*]
    And, Alexandro, let us honour thee
    With public notice of thy loyalty.
    To end those things articulated here   105
    By our great lord, the mighty King of Spain,

  80 *in kindness* by your nature (as a king)
  81 *fact* deed
  82 *our* my
  84 *suggestions* false accusations
  89 *misconceived* suspected, formed a wrong opinion of
  91 *Wherein* ed. (Or wherein *1592*)
  93 *doom* judgment
  98 *mean* moderate
 105 *articulated* contained in the proposals (or articles) sent by the
      King of Spain (see l.74)

We with our Council will deliberate.
Come, Alexandro, keep us company.   *Exeunt*

Act III, Scene ii

Enter HIERONIMO

HIERONIMO
O eyes, no eyes, but fountains fraught with tears;
O life, no life, but lively form of death;
O world, no world, but mass of public wrongs,
Confused and filled with murder and misdeeds!
O sacred heavens! if this unhallowed deed,   5
If this inhuman and barbarous attempt,
If this incomparable murder thus
Of mine, but now no more my son,
Shall unrevealed and unrevengéd pass,
How should we term your dealings to be just,   10
If you unjustly deal with those that in your justice trust?
The night, sad secretary to my moans,
With direful visions wake my vexed soul,
And with the wounds of my distressful son
Solicit me for notice of his death.   15
The ugly fiends do sally forth of hell,
And frame my steps to unfrequented paths,
And fear my heart with fierce inflamed thoughts.
The cloudy day my discontents records,
Early begins to register my dreams   20
And drive me forth to seek the murderer.

1 *fraught* filled
2 *lively form of death* death with the appearance of life
4 *Confused* disordered   12 *secretary* confidant
13 *wake* plural for singular; Edwards compares solicit (l.15) and
   drive (l.21)
14 *distressful* causing distress, or distressed
18 *fear* frighten

---

1 ff. When Bobadil and Matthew discuss plays (in *Everyman in his
   Humour*, I, iv) they reserve their highest (clownish) praise for this
   speech; and thus convey Jonson's scorn for Kyd's 'conceited' oratorical
   style (Jonson may himself have acted Hieronimo). Sympathetic modern
   critics think otherwise: Clemen's analysis (pp. 271–5) shows the speech
   as 'a masterpiece of rhetorical art. Its structure and proportions are
   worked out with an almost mathematical exactness, and a variety of
   stylistic figures are harmoniously dovetailed in order to make a powerful
   emotional impact.'

Eyes, life, world, heavens, hell, night, and day,
See, search, show, send some man, some mean, that may—
A letter falleth
What's here? a letter? tush, it is not so!
A letter written to Hieronimo!   *Red ink*   25
[*Reads*] ' For want of ink, receive this bloody writ.
Me hath my hapless brother hid from thee:
Revenge thyself on Balthazar and him,
For these were they that murderéd thy son.
Hieronimo, revenge Horatio's death,   30
And better fare than Bel-imperia doth.'
What means this unexpected miracle?
My son slain by Lorenzo and the prince!
What cause had they Horatio to malign?
Or what might move thee, Bel-imperia,   35
To accuse thy brother, had he been the mean?
Hieronimo, beware, thou art betrayed,
And to entrap thy life this train is laid.
Advise thee therefore, be not credulous:
This is devised to endanger thee,   40
That thou by this Lorenzo shouldst accuse,
And he, for thy dishonour done, should draw
Thy life in question, and thy name in hate.
Dear was the life of my beloved son,
And of his death behoves me be revenged: 45
Then hazard not thine own, Hieronimo,
But live t'effect thy resolution.
I therefore will by circumstances try
What I can gather to confirm this writ,
And, hearkening near the Duke of Castile's house,   50

23 *See . . . may—* ed. (See . . . some man, / Some . . . may: *1592*)
23 *mean* means, way   26 '*For* ed. (*Bel.* For *1592*)
26 *writ* writing, document
27 *hapless* luckless; perhaps 'attended with ill-luck'
32 *What* ed. (*Hiero* What *1592*)
34 *malign* hate   38 *train* plot, trap
47 *t'effect thy resolution* to bring about what you have resolved
48 *by circumstances* by observing how they act; by gathering circumstantial evidence

23 s.d. The pat arrival of the letter may be intended to emphasise how accident, under the direction of Revenge, favours the ultimate working-out of vengeance.
25 *Red ink* probably an author's note that the letter should be seen to have been written in red.

SCENE II]   THE SPANISH TRAGEDY   55

Close if I can with Bel-imperia,
To listen more, but nothing to bewray.

Enter PEDRINGANO

Now Pedringano!
PEDRINGANO   Now, Hieronimo!
HIERONIMO
Where's thy lady?
PEDRINGANO   I know not; here's my lord.

Enter LORENZO

LORENZO
How now, who's this? Hieronimo?
HIERONIMO   My lord.   55
PEDRINGANO
He asketh for my lady Bel-imperia.
LORENZO
What to do, Hieronimo? The duke my father hath
Upon some disgrace awhile removed her hence;
But if it be aught I may inform her of,
Tell me, Hieronimo, and I'll let her know it.   60
HIERONIMO
Nay, nay, my lord, I thank you, it shall not need.
I had a suit unto her, but too late,
And her disgrace makes me unfortunate.
LORENZO
Why so, Hieronimo? use me.
HIERONIMO
O no, my lord, I dare not, it must not be,   65
I humbly thank your lordship.
LORENZO   Why then, farewell.
HIERONIMO
My grief no heart, my thoughts no tongue can tell.

                                            Exit

LORENZO
Come hither, Pedringano, see'st thou this?
PEDRINGANO
My lord, I see it, and suspect it too.
LORENZO
This is that damned villain Serberine,   70
That hath, I fear, revealed Horatio's death.

51 *Close* meet; come to an understanding
52 *bewray* disclose   64 *use me* put your suit to me

PEDRINGANO

My lord, he could not, 'twas so lately done;
And since, he hath not left my company.

LORENZO

Admit he have not, his condition's such,
As fear or flattering words may make him false.   75
I know his humour, and therewith repent
That e'er I used him in this enterprise.
But Pedringano, to prevent the worst,
And 'cause I know thee secret as my soul,
Here, for thy further satisfaction, take thou this,   80
                              Gives him more gold
And hearken to me. Thus it is devised:
This night thou must, and prithee so resolve,
Meet Serberine at Saint Luigi's Park—
Thou know'st 'tis here hard by behind the house.
There take thy stand, and see thou strike him sure,   85
For die he must, if we do mean to live.

PEDRINGANO

But how shall Serberine be there, my lord?

LORENZO

Let me alone, I'll send to him to meet
The prince and me, where thou must do this deed.

PEDRINGANO

It shall be done, my lord, it shall be done,   90
And I'll go arm myself to meet him there.

LORENZO

When things shall alter, as I hope they will,
Then shalt thou mount for this: thou know'st my mind.
                              Exit PEDRINGANO

Che le Ieron!

74 *condition* nature, temperament   76 *humour* disposition
83 *Saint Luigi's* ed. (S. *Liugis 1592*)
88 *Let me alone* leave it to me
93 *mount* rise (socially); with a punning reference to 'mounting'
   the gallows, as he does; cf. II, iv, 60–1 on. Horatio's similar rise
94–7 lineation ed. (Goe . . . forthwith, / Meet . . . Parke, / Behinde . . .
   boy. *1592*)

---

94 *Che le Ieron!* unexplained; perhaps, as Boas suggests, a corruption
   of the page's name. Freeman (p. 68) offers the suggestion that 'Che le'
   is equivalent to Italian 'chi là' (Who [is] there?) and Ieron either the
   page's name or an abbreviation of Hieronimo; in the latter case the
   phrase would be prompted by Lorenzo's hearing a noise. This suggestion seems rather implausible dramatically.

Enter PAGE

PAGE   My lord?
LORENZO   Go, sirrah, to Serberine,
And bid him forthwith meet the prince and me   95
At Saint Luigi's Park, behind the house,
This evening, boy.
PAGE   I go, my lord.
LORENZO
But, sirrah, let the hour be eight o'clock.
Bid him not fail.
PAGE   I fly, my lord.   *Exit*
LORENZO
Now to confirm the complot thou hast cast   100
Of all these practices, I'll spread the watch,
Upon precise commandment from the king,
Strongly to guard the place where Pedringano
This night shall murder hapless Serberine.
Thus must we work that will avoid distrust,   105
Thus must we practise to prevent mishap,
And thus one ill another must expulse.
This sly enquiry of Hieronimo
For Bel-imperia breeds suspicion,
And this suspicion bodes a further ill.   110
As for myself, I know my secret fault;
And so do they, but I have dealt for them.
They that for coin their souls endangered,
To save my life, for coin shall venture theirs:
And better it's that base companions die,   115
Than by their life to hazard our good haps.
Nor shall they live, for me to fear their faith:

96 *Saint Luigi's* ed. (*S. Liugis 1592*)
100 *complot* conspiracy
100 *cast* devised
101 *practices* deceits, plots
101 *spread the watch* position the constables
105 *distrust* suspicion
106 *practise* scheme
107 *expulse* expel
108–9 lineation ed. (This . . . suspition, *one line 1592*)
115 *it's* ed. (its *1592*) 115 *base companions* low-bred vulgar fellows
116 *good haps* good fortune, security
117 *fear their faith* be apprehensive about their keeping faith

105–19 a speech full of sentiments typical of the Elizabethan 'Machiavellian'.

I'll trust myself, myself shall be my friend,
For die they shall, slaves are ordained to no other end.

Exit

Act III, Scene iii

Enter PEDRINGANO *with a pistol*

PEDRINGANO
Now, Pedringano, bid thy pistol hold,
And hold on, Fortune! once more favour me;
Give but success to mine attempting spirit,
And let me shift for taking of mine aim!
Here is the gold, this is the gold proposed: 5
It is no dream that I adventure for,
But Pedringano is possessed thereof.
And he that would not strain his conscience
For him that thus his liberal purse hath stretched,
Unworthy such a favour may he fail,   10
And, wishing, want, when such as I prevail.
As for the fear of apprehension,
I know, if need should be, my noble lord
Will stand between me and ensuing harms;
Besides, this place is free from all suspect.   15
Here therefore will I stay and take my stand.

Enter the WATCH

1 WATCH
I wonder much to what intent it is
That we are thus expressly charged to watch.
2 WATCH
'Tis by commandment in the king's own name.
3 WATCH
But we were never wont to watch and ward   20
So near the duke his brother's house before.

119 *slaves* mean, worthless fellows
  1 *hold* be true, function properly
  2 *hold on* continue, be consistent
  4 *let me shift* leave it to me
  7 *is possessed thereof* actually has the gold in his grasp
 10 *fail* be unsuccessful, fall into poverty
 15 *suspect* suspicion
 20 *watch and ward* patrol, keep guard. 'Originally part of the legal
    definition of the duties of a sentinel' (Edwards)

2 WATCH
    Content yourself, stand close, there's somewhat in't.

Enter SERBERINE

SERBERINE
    Here, Serberine, attend and stay thy pace,
    For here did Don Lorenzo's page appoint
    That thou by his command shouldst meet with him.   25
    How fit a place, if one were so disposed,
    Methinks this corner is, to close with one.
PEDRINGANO
    Here comes the bird that I must seize upon;
    Now, Pedringano, or never, play the man!
SERBERINE
    I wonder that his lordship stays so long,   30
    Or wherefore should he send for me so late?
PEDRINGANO
    For this, Serberine, and thou shalt ha't.

                                        Shoots the dag
    So, there he lies, my promise is performed.

                    The WATCH

1 WATCH
    Hark gentlemen, this is a pistol shot.
2 WATCH
    And here's one slain; stay the murderer.   35
PEDRINGANO
    Now by the sorrows of the souls in hell,
                        He strives with the WATCH
    Who first lays hand on me, I'll be his priest.
3 WATCH
    Sirrah, confess, and therein play the priest;
    Why hast thou thus unkindly killed the man?
PEDRINGANO
    Why? because he walked abroad so late.   40

22 *close* concealed
23 *stay thy pace* cease walking
27 *close with* grapple with, attack at close quarters (*O.E.D.*, v, 13)
32 s.d. *dag* a heavy pistol
35 *stay* arrest
37 *I'll be his priest* i.e. I'll be there at his death; I'll make an end of
    him
39 *unkindly* inhumanly, against nature
40 *abroad* out of doors

3 WATCH
  Come sir, you had been better kept your bed,
  Than have committed this misdeed so late.
2 WATCH
  Come, to the marshal's with the murderer!
1 WATCH
  On to Hieronimo's! help me here
  To bring the murdered body with us too.   45
PEDRINGANO
  Hieronimo? carry me before whom you will,
  Whate'er he be I'll answer him and you.
  And do your worst, for I defy you all.   *Exeunt*

Act III, Scene iv

Enter LORENZO *and* BALTHAZAR

BALTHAZAR
  How now, my lord, what makes you rise so soon?
LORENZO
  Fear of preventing our mishaps too late.
BALTHAZAR
  What mischief is it that we not mistrust?
LORENZO
  Our greatest ills we least mistrust, my lord,
  And inexpected harms do hurt us most.   5
BALTHAZAR
  Why tell me Don Lorenzo, tell me man,
  If aught concerns our honour and your own.
LORENZO
  Nor you nor me, my lord, but both in one;
  For I suspect, and the presumption's great,
  That by those base confederates in our fault   10
  Touching the death of Don Horatio,
  We are betrayed to old Hieronimo.
BALTHAZAR
  Betrayed, Lorenzo? tush, it cannot be.
LORENZO
  A guilty conscience, urged with the thought

  43 *Come,* ed. (Come *1592*)
   2 *preventing* forestalling
   3 *mistrust* 'suspect the existence of or anticipate the occurrence of
     [something evil]' (*O.E.D.*, v, 3)
   5 *inexpected* ed. (in expected *1592*)
  10 *confederates in our fault* partners in crime

Of former evils, easily cannot err: 15
I am persuaded, and dissuade me not,
That all's revealed to Hieronimo.
And therefore know that I have cast it thus—

[*Enter* PAGE]

But here's the page. How now, what news with thee?
PAGE
My lord, Serberine is slain.   20
BALTHAZAR
Who? Serberine, my man?
PAGE
Your highness' man, my lord.
LORENZO
Speak page, who murdered him?
PAGE
He that is apprehended for the fact.
LORENZO
Who?   25
PAGE
Pedringano.
BALTHAZAR
Is Serberine slain, that loved his lord so well?
Injurious villain, murderer of his friend!
LORENZO
Hath Pedringano murdered Serberine?
My lord, let me entreat you to take the pains   30
To exasperate and hasten his revenge
With your complaints unto my lord the king.
This their dissension breeds a greater doubt.
BALTHAZAR
Assure thee, Don Lorenzo, he shall die,
Or else his highness hardly shall deny.   35
Meanwhile I'll haste the Marshal-Sessions,
For die he shall for this his damned deed.

Exit BALTHAZAR

18 *cast it thus* laid these plans
24 *fact* deed, crime
31 *exasperate* make harsher
32 *complaints* outcries, statements of grievance
33 *doubt* fear
35 *hardly shall deny* either 'refuse only with difficulty' or (as Edwards suggests) 'show harshness in denying me'

4

LORENZO

Why so, this fits our former policy,
And thus experience bids the wise to deal:
I lay the plot, he prosecutes the point;   40
I set the trap, he breaks the worthless twigs,
And sees not that wherewith the bird was limed.
Thus hopeful men, that mean to hold their own,
Must look like fowlers to their dearest friends.
He runs to kill whom I have holp to catch,   45
And no man knows it was my reaching fatch.
'Tis hard to trust unto a multitude,
Or anyone, in mine opinion,
When men themselves their secrets will reveal.

Enter a MESSENGER *with a letter*

Boy!   50

PAGE

My lord?

LORENZO

What's he?

MESSENGER   I have a letter to your lordship.

LORENZO

From whence?

MESSENGER   From Pedringano that's imprisoned.

LORENZO

So he is in prison then?

MESSENGER   Ay, my good lord.

LORENZO

What would he with us? He writes us here   55
To stand good lord and help him in distress.
Tell him I have his letters, know his mind,
And what we may, let him assure him of.
Fellow, begone: my boy shall follow thee.

Exit MESSENGER

40 *prosecutes the point* brings about the goal aimed at
42 *limed* caught in bird-lime   45 *holp* helped
46 *reaching* penetrating, designing
46 *fatch* stratagem (equals 'fetch', *O.E.D.*, sb.1, 2)
55–6 lineation ed. (What . . . vs? / He . . . distres. *1592*)
56 *stand good lord* act as good lord and protector

38–49 another typical speech of Machiavellian 'policy', where the main
aim was to manipulate others.

This works like wax; yet once more try thy wits.　60
Boy, go convey this purse to Pedringano,
Thou knowest the prison, closely give it him,
And be advised that none be there about.
Bid him be merry still, but secret;
And though the Marshal-Sessions be today,　65
Bid him not doubt of his delivery.
Tell him his pardon is already signed,
And thereon bid him boldly be resolved;
For, were he ready to be turned off
(As 'tis my will the uttermost be tried)　70
Thou with his pardon shalt attend him still.
Show him this box, tell him his pardon's in't,
But open't not, and if thou lov'st thy life,
But let him wisely keep his hopes unknown;
He shall not want while Don Lorenzo lives.　75
Away!
PAGE　　I go my lord, I run.
LORENZO
But sirrah, see that this be cleanly done.　　*Exit* PAGE
Now stands our fortune on a tickle point,
And now or never ends Lorenzo's doubts.
One only thing is uneffected yet,　80
And that's to see the executioner.
But to what end? I list not trust the air
With utterance of our pretence therein,
For fear the privy whispering of the wind
Convey our words amongst unfriendly ears,　85
That lie too open to advantages.
E quel che voglio io, nessun lo sa,
Intendo io: quel mi basterà.　　*Exit*

60 *works like wax* follows my design (as wax is easily moulded and
　　formed)
62 *closely* secretly　　　　63 *be advised* take care
68 *boldly be resolved* feel completely assured
69 *turned off* hanged (the prisoner is 'turned off' the support he
　　stands on and so hanged; see III, vi, 104 s.d.)
73 *and if* if　　　　75–6 lineation ed. (*one line 1592*)
77 *cleanly* efficiently　　　　78 *tickle* precarious, finely-balanced
79 *doubts* fears　　　　82 *list not* have no wish to
83 *pretence* design, intention
86 *advantages* taking advantage, getting the upper hand
87–8 *E quel . . . basterà* ed. (*Et quel que voglio Ii nessun le sa,/Intendo*
　　io quel mi bassara. 1592) 'And what I wish, no one knows; *I*
　　understand, that suffices me'

Act III, Scene v

Enter BOY *with the box*

PAGE

My master hath forbidden me to look in this box, and by my
troth 'tis likely, if he had not warned me, I should not have
had so much idle time; for we men's-kind in our minority are
like women in their uncertainty: that they are most forbidden, they will soonest attempt. So I now. By my bare   5
honesty, here's nothing but the bare empty box. Were it not
sin against secrecy, I would say it were a piece of gentleman-
like knavery. I must go to Pedringano, and tell him his
pardon is in this box; nay, I would have sworn it, had I not
seen the contrary. I cannot choose but smile to think how   10
the villain will flout the gallows, scorn the audience, and
descant on the hangman, and all presuming of his pardon
from hence. Will't not be an odd jest, for me to stand and
grace every jest he makes, pointing my finger at this box, as
who would say, 'Mock on, here's thy warrant'. Is't not a   15
scurvy jest that a man should jest himself to death? Alas,
poor Pedringano, I am in a sort sorry for thee, but if I should
be hanged with thee, I cannot weep.   *Exit*

Act III, Scene vi

Enter HIERONIMO *and the* DEPUTY

HIERONIMO

Thus must we toil in other men's extremes,
That know not how to remedy our own;
And do them justice, when unjustly we,

1 s.p. PAGE ed. (*not in 1592*)
3 *minority* while still boys   4 *uncertainty* fearfulness
11 *flout* jest at   12 *descant on* hold forth about
16 *scurvy* bitter, base
1 s.d. DEPUTY 'the official title of the assistant to the Knight
Marshal' (Edwards)
1 *extremes* difficulties, hardships

1 ff. This speech, and that at III, vii, 10 ff., is crucial to an understanding
   of Hieronimo's outlook at this stage in the play. Both speeches show,
   against hostile critics, Hieronimo's deep concern for justice (and not
   merely vengeance), together with his frustration at Heaven's apparent
   deafness.

For all our wrongs, can compass no redress.
But shall I never live to see the day   5
That I may come, by justice of the heavens,
To know the cause that may my cares allay?
This toils my body, this consumeth age,
That only I to all men just must be,
And neither gods nor men be just to me.   10

DEPUTY
Worthy Hieronimo, your office asks
A care to punish such as do transgress.

HIERONIMO
So is't my duty to regard his death
Who when he lived deserved my dearest blood.
But come, for that we came for, let's begin,   15
For here lies that which bids me to be gone.

Enter OFFICERS, BOY, *and* PEDRINGANO, *with a letter in his hand,*
bound

DEPUTY
Bring forth the prisoner, for the court is set.

PEDRINGANO
Gramercy, boy, but it was time to come;
For I had written to my lord anew
A nearer matter that concerneth him,   20
For fear his lordship had forgotten me.
But sith he hath remembered me so well—
Come, come, come on, when shall we to this gear?

HIERONIMO
Stand forth, thou monster, murderer of men,
And here, for satisfaction of the world,   25
Confess thy folly and repent thy fault,
For there's thy place of execution.

7 *know the cause* experience the circumstance
8 *toils* burdens   8 *consumeth age* wears out my life
13 *regard* care about, concern myself with
14 *deserved* merited my spilling
15 ed. (But come, for that we came for lets begin, *1592*)
18 *Gramercy* an exclamation of relief
20 *nearer* of greater concern, more serious
23 *gear* business
25 *for satisfaction of* to convince, demonstrate to

16 *here* Hieronimo touches his head or heart. Or possibly (as Boas thinks)
he refers to the bloody handkercher.

PEDRINGANO
   This is short work! Well, to your marshalship
   First I confess, nor fear I death therefore,
   I am the man, 'twas I slew Serberine.   30
   But sir, then you think this shall be the place
   Where we shall satisfy you for this gear?

DEPUTY
   Ay, Pedringano.

PEDRINGANO   Now I think not so.

HIERONIMO
   Peace, impudent, for thou shalt find it so:
   For blood with blood shall, while I sit as judge,   35
   Be satisfied, and the law discharged.
   And though myself cannot receive the like,
   Yet will I see that others have their right.
   Despatch, the fault's approvéd and confessed,
   And by our law he is condemned to die.   40

HANGMAN
   Come on sir, are you ready?

PEDRINGANO
   To do what, my fine officious knave?

HANGMAN
   To go to this gear.

PEDRINGANO
   O sir, you are too forward; thou wouldst fain furnish me
   with a halter, to disfurnish me of my habit. So I should go   45
   out of this gear, my raiment, into that gear, the rope. But,
   hangman, now I spy your knavery, I'll not change without
   boot, that's flat.

HANGMAN
   Come sir.

PEDRINGANO
   So then, I must up?   50

29 *therefore* 'therefor' may be the correct reading
32 *gear* action, behaviour
39 *approvéd* proved, shown openly
43 *this gear* i.e. hanging
44 *forward* presumptuous
44–8 prose ed. (O sir . . . habit. / So . . . rope. / But . . . flat. *1592*)
45 *habit* clothes
47–8 *without boot* without compensation, without some amends
    (*O.E.D.*, sb. 19)

---

45 *disfurnish me of my habit* Pedringano refers to the custom of giving the
hangman his victim's clothes.

HANGMAN
   No remedy.
PEDRINGANO
   Yes, but there shall be for my coming down.
HANGMAN
   Indeed, here's a remedy for that.
PEDRINGANO
   How? be turned off?
HANGMAN
   Ay, truly; come, are you ready? I pray, sir, despatch, the   55
   day goes away.
PEDRINGANO
   What, do you hang by the hour? If you do, I may chance to
   break your old custom.
HANGMAN
   Faith, you have reason, for I am like to break your young
   neck.   60
PEDRINGANO
   Dost thou mock me, hangman? Pray God I be not preserved
   to break your knave's pate for this.
HANGMAN
   Alas, sir, you are a foot too low to reach it, and I hope you
   will never grow so high while I am in the office.
PEDRINGANO
   Sirrah, dost see yonder boy with the box in his hand?   65
HANGMAN
   What, he that points to it with his finger?
PEDRINGANO
   Ay, that companion.
HANGMAN
   I know him not, but what of him?
PEDRINGANO
   Dost thou think to live till his old doublet will make thee a
   new truss?   70
HANGMAN
   Ay, and many a fair year after, to truss up many an honester
   man than either thou or he.

54 *turned off* be thrust off the support and so hang
55 *despatch* work quickly
55–6 as prose ed. (I . . . ready / I . . . away. *1592*)
57 *by the hour* at set times
67 *companion* fellow
70 *truss* a close-fitting jacket (*O.E.D.*, sb. 3a); to 'truss up' (l.71) is to
    hang

PEDRINGANO

What hath he in his box, as thou think'st?

HANGMAN

Faith, I cannot tell, nor I care not greatly. Methinks you
should rather hearken to your soul's health.   75

PEDRINGANO

Why, sirrah hangman, I take it that that is good for the body
is likewise good for the soul; and it may be, in that box is
balm for both.

HANGMAN

Well, thou art even the merriest piece of man's flesh that
e'er groaned at my office door.   80

PEDRINGANO

Is your roguery become an 'office' with a knave's name?

HANGMAN

Ay, and that shall all they witness that see you seal it with a
thief's name.

PEDRINGANO

I prithee, request this good company to pray with me.

HANGMAN

Ay marry sir, this is a good motion; my masters, you see   85
here's a good fellow.

PEDRINGANO

Nay, nay, now I remember me, let them alone till some other
time, for now I have no great need.

HIERONIMO

I have not seen a wretch so impudent!
O monstrous times, where murder's set so light;   90
And where the soul that should be shrined in heaven,
Solely delights in interdicted things,
Still wandering in the thorny passages
That intercepts itself of happiness.
Murder, O bloody monster, God forbid   95
A fault so foul should 'scape unpunished.

75 *hearken to* care for
74–5 as prose ed. (Faith . . . greatly. / Me thinks . . . health. *1592*)
85 *motion* suggestion, idea
93 *Still* always, for ever

---

81 *Is your . . . 'office'* Pedringano mocks the high-sounding 'office' used to
describe the hangman's low-born ('knave's') occupation.
94 Edwards explains 'which prevent it (the soul) from attaining happiness.'
A more natural construction would arise if 'That' were a misprint
for 'And', making 'soul' the subject of 'intercepts'; there are, however,
no grounds for emendation.

Despatch and see this execution done—
This makes me to remember thee, my son.

Exit HIERONIMO

PEDRINGANO
Nay soft, no haste.
DEPUTY
Why, wherefore stay you? Have you hope of life?   100
PEDRINGANO
Why, ay.
HANGMAN
As how?
PEDRINGANO
Why, rascal, by my pardon from the king.
HANGMAN
Stand you on that? then you shall off with this.

He turns him off

DEPUTY
So, executioner. Convey him hence,   105
But let his body be unburied:
Let not the earth be choked or infect
With that which heaven contemns, and men neglect.

Exeunt

Act III, Scene vii

Enter HIERONIMO

HIERONIMO
Where shall I run to breathe abroad my woes,
My woes whose weight hath wearied the earth?

 99 *soft* wait a moment
104 *Stand you on that?* Do you depend on that? The hangman then
    refers to the literal sense of 'stand'
108 *heaven* ed. (heauens *1592*)
  1 s.p. HIERONIMO ed. (*not in 1592*)
  1 *breathe abroad* give expression to

104 s.d. The property which has already done duty as an arbour may have
     again been used here (stripped, perhaps, of its leaves and branches)
     to effect this second hanging. But see II, iv, 53 s.d. and note.
  1–9 Hieronimo's language, and the implied stage-action, may seem
     exaggerated and over-theatrical to modern readers; the speech is,
     however, very nicely calculated for stage-delivery and may be played
     with restraint, while the wording very effectively conveys Hieronimo's
     total preoccupation with his son's death.

Or mine exclaims, that have surcharged the air
With ceaseless plaints for my deceased son?
The blustering winds, conspiring with my words,   5
At my lament have moved the leafless trees,
Disrobed the meadows of their flowered green,
Made mountains marsh with spring-tides of my tears,
And broken through the brazen gates of hell.
Yet still tormented is my tortured soul   10
With broken sighs and restless passions,
That winged mount, and hovering in the air,
Beat at the windows of the brightest heavens,
Soliciting for justice and revenge;
But they are placed in those empyreal heights,   15
Where, counter-mured with walls of diamond,
I find the place impregnable; and they
Resist my woes, and give my words no way.

Enter HANGMAN *with a letter*

HANGMAN
O lord sir, God bless you sir, the man sir,
Petergade sir, he that was so full of merry conceits—   20
HIERONIMO
Well, what of him?
HANGMAN
O lord sir, he went the wrong way, the fellow had a fair
commission to the contrary. Sir, here is his passport; I pray
you sir, we have done him wrong.
HIERONIMO
I warrant thee, give it me.   25
HANGMAN
You will stand between the gallows and me?
HIERONIMO
Ay, ay.

   3 *exclaims* cries
   11 *passions* sufferings, protesting cries
   15 *empyreal* of the highest heaven; the dwelling-place of God
   16 *counter-mured* having two walls, one within the other
   20 *Petergade* the hangman's bungling attempt at 'Pedringano'
   20 *conceits* jests
   22–3 *fair commission* proper written authority

10–18 Hieronimo's sense of thwarted right, and the apparent indifference
   of 'the brightest heavens', are main elements in our sympathy for his
   cause. His state of mind predicts, if briefly and unsubtly, the baffled and
   thwarted questioning of Hamlet.

HANGMAN
  I thank your Lord Worship.

                                              Exit HANGMAN
HIERONIMO
  And yet, though somewhat nearer me concerns,
  I will, to ease the grief that I sustain,   30
  Take truce with sorrow while I read on this.
  'My lord, I writ as mine extremes required,
  That you would labour my delivery;
  If you neglect, my life is desperate,
  And in my death I shall reveal the troth.   35
  You know, my lord, I slew him for your sake;
  And as confederate with the prince and you,
  Won by rewards and hopeful promises,
  I holp to murder Don Horatio too.'
  Holp he to murder mine Horatio?   40
  And actors in th' accursed tragedy
  Wast thou, Lorenzo, Balthazar and thou,
  Of whom my son, my son deserved so well?
  What have I heard, what have mine eyes beheld?
  O sacred heavens, may it come to pass   45
  That such a monstrous and detested deed,
  So closely smothered, and so long concealed,
  Shall thus by this be vengéd or revealed!
  Now see I what I durst not then suspect,
  That Bel-imperia's letter was not feigned.   50
  Nor feigned she, though falsely they have wronged
  Both her, myself, Horatio and themselves.

32 *writ* ed. (write *1592*)
32 *extremes* extreme position, predicament
34 *desperate* despaired of, without hope
37 *as* ed. (was *1592*)
47 *closely smothered* kept a close secret

---

32 *writ* The past tense (see textual gloss) must be correct; Pedringano
    refers to his *previous* letter.
37 *as confederate* Edwards's correction ('as' for 'was') gives good sense and
    syntax; Joseph's retention of 'was' on the grounds that three separate
    statements are involved is possible but strained.
45 ff. Hieronimo accepts that coincidences indicate Heaven's wish to bring
    about justice; a weakened form of the mediaeval belief in Fortune as
    God's servant.
50-1 *was not feigned. Nor feigned she* 'He is relieved of two doubts [see
    III, ii, 37-52], whether or not Bel-imperia really wrote the letter, and if
    so whether or not she was telling the truth.' (McIlwraith.)

Now may I make compare, 'twixt hers and this,
Of every accident; I ne'er could find
Till now, and now I feelingly perceive,   55
They did what heaven unpunished would not leave.
O false Lorenzo, are these thy flattering looks?
Is this the honour that thou didst my son?
And Balthazar, bane to thy soul and me,
Was this the ransom he reserved thee for?   60
Woe to the cause of these constrained wars,
Woe to thy baseness and captivity,
Woe to thy birth, thy body and thy soul,
Thy cursed father, and thy conquered self!
And banned with bitter execrations be   65
The day and place where he did pity thee!
But wherefore waste I mine unfruitful words,
When naught but blood will satisfy my woes?
I will go plain me to my lord the king,
And cry aloud for justice through the court,   70
Wearing the flints with these my withered feet,
And either purchase justice by entreats
Or tire them all with my revenging threats.   *Exit*

Act III, Scene viii

Enter ISABELLA *and her* MAID

ISABELLA
So that, you say, this herb will purge the eye,
And this the head?

54 *accident;* ed. (accident, *1592*) happening, occurrence (relating to
   Horatio's death)
54 *find* understand   55 *feelingly* vividly, with feeling
59 *bane* poison, cause of ruin   61 *constrained* forced, unnecessary
65 *banned* cursed   69 *plain* complain, plead
 1 *purge* cleanse, heal
 2-3 lineation ed. (*one line 1592*)

53-6 'Now I can check on every happening, by using the two letters;
   I could never be sure till now — but now I see very vividly — that
   they committed this crime which Heaven must and will punish.'
   Edwards, I take it, is correct in keeping (and giving greater weight to)
   1592's stop after 'accident'.
69-73 Hieronimo's impulse is to seek justice through the approved
   channels; only if he is thwarted will he take matters into his own hands.
 1-5 These lines may conceivably have suggested Ophelia's flower-lore
   in madness.

Ah, but none of them will purge the heart:
No, there's no medicine left for my disease,
Nor any physic to recure the dead.   5

She runs lunatic

Horatio! O, where's Horatio?

MAID

Good madam, affright not thus yourself
With outrage for your son Horatio:
He sleeps in quiet in the Elysian fields.

ISABELLA

Why, did I not give you gowns and goodly things,   10
Bought you a whistle and a whipstalk too,
To be revenged on their villainies?

MAID

Madam, these humours do torment my soul.

ISABELLA

My soul! poor soul, thou talks of things
Thou know'st not what—my soul hath silver wings,   15
That mounts me up unto the highest heavens;
To heaven, ay, there sits my Horatio,
Backed with a troop of fiery cherubins,
Dancing about his newly-healed wounds,
Singing sweet hymns and chanting heavenly notes,   20
Rare harmony to greet his innocence,
That died, ay died a mirror in our days.
But say, where shall I find the men, the murderers,
That slew Horatio? Whither shall I run
To find them out that murdered my son?   *Exeunt* 25

---

5 *recure* recover, restore to health
8 *outrage* outrageous behaviour, passion
9 *Elysian fields* the place of the blessed in the afterworld
11 *whipstalk* whip-handle; used, presumably, in a child's game
13 *humours* uncontrolled fancies
21 *greet* honour (*not*, as the context shows, 'welcome'); Edwards
   compares (*O.E.D.*, 3e) Spenser's use of the word to mean 'to offer
   congratulations'
22 *mirror* model of excellence

14–22 Isabella's language here, perhaps only to secure pathos, is distinctly
   Christian in its description of the after-life, in contrast to the Vergilian
   language of most other references. Edwards has shown that Kyd's
   writing here may be indebted to Thomas Watson's elegy on Walsingham, published in 1590.

Act III, Scene ix

BEL-IMPERIA *at a window*

BEL-IMPERIA
    What means this outrage that is offered me?
    Why am I thus sequestered from the court?
    No notice? Shall I not know the cause
    Of this my secret and suspicious ills?
    Accursed brother, unkind murderer,   5
    Why bends thou thus thy mind to martyr me?
    Hieronimo, why writ I of thy wrongs,
    Or why art thou so slack in thy revenge?
    Andrea, O Andrea, that thou sawest
    Me for thy friend Horatio handled thus,   10
    And him for me thus causeless murdered.
    Well, force perforce, I must constrain myself
    To patience, and apply me to the time,
    Till heaven, as I have hoped, shall set me free.
                    Enter CHRISTOPHIL
CHRISTOPHIL
    Come, Madam Bel-imperia, this may not be.   *Exeunt*   15

Act III, Scene x

Enter LORENZO, BALTHAZAR, *and the* PAGE

LORENZO
    Boy, talk no further, thus far things go well.
    Thou art assured that thou sawest him dead?
PAGE
    Or else my lord I live not.
LORENZO   That's enough.
    As for his resolution in his end,
    Leave that to him with whom he sojourns now.   5
    Here, take my ring and give it Christophil,

    2 *sequestered* kept apart, secluded
    3 *No notice* kept in ignorance
    4 *suspicious* arousing suspicion
    5 *unkind* unnatural
    6 *bends* applies
    12 *force perforce* of necessity
    13 *apply me to the time* accept things as they are
    4 *resolution* courage

And bid him let my sister be enlarged,
And bring her hither straight.   *Exit* PAGE
This that I did was for a policy
To smooth and keep the murder secret,   10
Which as a nine-days' wonder being o'erblown,
My gentle sister will I now enlarge.

BALTHAZAR

And time, Lorenzo, for my lord the duke,
You heard, enquired for her yester-night.

LORENZO

Why, and, my lord, I hope you heard me say   15
Sufficient reason why she kept away.
But that's all one. My lord, you love her?

BALTHAZAR   Ay.

LORENZO

Then in your love beware, deal cunningly,
Salve all suspicions; only soothe me up;
And if she hap to stand on terms with us,   20
As for her sweetheart, and concealment so,
Jest with her gently: under feigned jest
Are things concealed that else would breed unrest.
But here she comes.

Enter BEL-IMPERIA

Now, sister—

BEL-IMPERIA   Sister? No!
Thou art no brother, but an enemy,   25
Else wouldst thou not have used thy sister so:
First, to affright me with thy weapons drawn,
And with extremes abuse my company;
And then to hurry me, like whirlwind's rage,
Amidst a crew of thy confederates,   30
And clap me up where none might come at me,

---

7 *enlarged* set free
9 *policy* stratagem, cunning purpose
10 *smooth* avoid difficult consequences
19 *Salve* allay
19 *soothe me up* agree with me
20 *stand on terms* argue, prove difficult
24 *Now* ed. (*Lor.* Now *1592*)
24–5 lineation ed. (But . . . comes. / Now Sister. / Sister . . . enemy.
    1592)
28 *extremes* harsh behaviour
31 *clap me up* lock me up, unceremoniously

Nor I at any, to reveal my wrongs.
What madding fury did possess thy wits?
Or wherein is't that I offended thee?

LORENZO
Advise you better, Bel-imperia,   35
For I have done you no disparagement;
Unless, by more discretion than deserved,
I sought to save your honour and mine own.

BEL-IMPERIA
Mine honour! why, Lorenzo, wherein is't
That I neglect my reputation so,   40
As you, or any, need to rescue it?

LORENZO
His highness and my father were resolved
To come confer with old Hieronimo,
Concerning certain matters of estate,
That by the viceroy was determined.   45

BEL-IMPERIA
And wherein was mine honour touched in that?

BALTHAZAR
Have patience, Bel-imperia; hear the rest.

LORENZO
Me next in sight as messenger they sent,
To give him notice that they were so nigh:
Now when I came, consorted with the prince,   50
And unexpected, in an arbour there,
Found Bel-imperia with Horatio—

BEL-IMPERIA
How then?

LORENZO
Why then, remembering that old disgrace,
Which you for Don Andrea had endured,   55
And now were likely longer to sustain,

36 *disparagement* dishonour, humiliation
48 *next in sight* standing nearby

---

37 'unless it were that, showing more concern and foresight than you
  deserved . . . '
44–5 Edwards, citing *O.E.D.*, explains: 'concerning certain matters about
  possessions which the viceroy had given up.' 'determined' might,
  however, mean more simply 'decided' or 'specified', and 'matters of
  estate' might mean 'matters of importance', 'state-matters'.
54 *that old disgrace* See I, i, 10–11 and note.

By being found so meanly accompanied,
Thought rather, for I knew no readier mean,
To thrust Horatio forth my father's way.

BALTHAZAR

And carry you obscurely somewhere else,   60
Lest that his highness should have found you there.

BEL-IMPERIA

Even so, my lord? And you are witness
That this is true which he entreateth of?
You, gentle brother, forged this for my sake,
And you, my lord, were made his instrument: 65
A work of worth, worthy the noting too!
But what's the cause that you concealed me since?

LORENZO

Your melancholy, sister, since the news
Of your first favourite Don Andrea's death,
My father's old wrath hath exasperate.   70

BALTHAZAR

And better was't for you, being in disgrace,
To absent yourself, and give his fury place.

BEL-IMPERIA

But why had I no notice of his ire?

LORENZO

That were to add more fuel to your fire,
Who burnt like Aetna for Andrea's loss.   75

BEL-IMPERIA

Hath not my father then enquired for me?

LORENZO

Sister, he hath, and thus excused I thee.

                                    He whispereth in her ear

But, Bel-imperia, see the gentle prince;
Look on thy love, behold young Balthazar,
Whose passions by thy presence are increased;   80
And in whose melancholy thou may'st see
Thy hate, his love; thy flight, his following thee.

57 *meanly* by a man of low rank
64 *forged* devised and executed this course of action; with an ironic
   hint of the modern sense of deceit
70 *exasperate* made harsher
72 *give his fury place* allow his wrath to expend itself harmlessly
75 *Aetna* the volcano in Sicily

57 *so meanly accompanied* Horatio's inferior social standing is frequently
   emphasised.

BEL-IMPERIA
    Brother, you are become an orator—
    I know not, I, by what experience—
    Too politic for me, past all compare,   85
    Since last I saw you; but content yourself,
    The prince is meditating higher things.
BALTHAZAR
    'Tis of thy beauty, then, that conquers kings;
    Of those thy tresses, Ariadne's twines,
    Wherewith my liberty thou hast surprised;   90
    Of that thine ivory front, my sorrow's map,
    Wherein I see no haven to rest my hope.
BEL-IMPERIA
    To love and fear, and both at once, my lord,
    In my conceit, are things of more import
    Than women's wits are to be busied with.   95
BALTHAZAR
    'Tis I that love.
BEL-IMPERIA   Whom?
BALTHAZAR   Bel-imperia.
BEL-IMPERIA
    But I that fear.
BALTHAZAR   Whom?
BEL-IMPERIA   Bel-imperia.
LORENZO
    Fear yourself?
BEL-IMPERIA   Ay, brother.
LORENZO   How?
BEL-IMPERIA   As those
    That what they love are loath and fear to lose.

---

89 *twines* threads, cords
90 *surprised* captured
91 *front* forehead
94 *In my conceit* to my mind, in my judgment
98–9 lineation ed. (*one line 1592*)

---

85 *Too politic* refers to the 'orator' (who has become too cunning), and not
   to 'experience'.
89 *Ariadne's* Kyd probably has in mind here Arachne, the Lydian weaver
   whom Athene changed to a spider; Ariadne, daughter of King Minos
   of Crete, did, however, use a thread in guiding Theseus through the
   labyrinth. Neither is especially apt here.
91 *sorrow's map* the forehead was supposed to reflect feelings; it is a 'map'
   because Balthazar seeks its aid in discovering the success of his proposal.

BALTHAZAR
  Then, fair, let Balthazar your keeper be.   100
BEL-IMPERIA
  No, Balthazar doth fear as well as we:
  Et tremulo metui pavidum junxere timorem,
  Et vanum stolidae proditionis opus.   *Exit*
LORENZO
  Nay, and you argue things so cunningly,
  We'll go continue this discourse at court.   105
BALTHAZAR
  Led by the loadstar of her heavenly looks,
  Wends poor oppressed Balthazar,
  As o'er the mountains walks the wanderer,
  Incertain to effect his pilgrimage.   *Exeunt*

Act III, Scene xi

Enter two PORTINGALES, *and* HIERONIMO *meets them*

1 PORTINGALE
  By your leave, sir.
HIERONIMO
  Good leave have you: nay, I pray you go,
  For I'll leave you; if you can leave me, so.
2 PORTINGALE
  Pray you, which is the next way to my lord the duke's?
HIERONIMO
  The next way from me.
1 PORTINGALE   To his house, we mean.   5
HIERONIMO
  O, hard by, 'tis yon house that you see.
2 PORTINGALE
  You could not tell us if his son were there?

102 *Et* ed. (*Est 1592*)
106 *loadstar* a star to steer by, usually in reference to the pole-star
109 *Incertain to effect* with no confidence of being able to complete
  3 *me, so* ed. (me so *1592*)
  4 *next* nearest

102-3 'They yoked craven fear to trembling dread: and that a fruitless
    work of doltish treason'. It is difficult to make of these lines a more than
    very general sense.
  1-8 Hieronimo's inconsequential talk, like Hamlet's 'wild and whirling
    words', is meant to convey the tension he is suffering under. The
    'Third Addition', inserted after l.1, much expands this state of mind.

HIERONIMO
   Who, my lord Lorenzo?
1 PORTINGALE   Ay, sir.
            He goeth in at one door and comes out at another
HIERONIMO   O, forbear,
   For other talk for us far fitter were.
   But if you be importunate to know   10
   The way to him, and where to find him out,
   Then list to me, and I'll resolve your doubt.
   There is a path upon your left-hand side,
   That leadeth from a guilty conscience
   Unto a forest of distrust and fear,   15
   A darksome place, and dangerous to pass:
   There shall you meet with melancholy thoughts,
   Whose baleful humours if you but uphold,
   It will conduct you to despair and death;
   Whose rocky cliffs when you have once beheld,   20
   Within a hugy dale of lasting night,
   That, kindled with the world's iniquities,
   Doth cast up filthy and detested fumes,
   Not far from thence, where murderers have built
   A habitation for their cursed souls,   25
   There, in a brazen cauldron, fixed by Jove
   In his fell wrath upon a sulphur flame,
   Yourselves shall find Lorenzo bathing him
   In boiling lead and blood of innocents.
1 PORTINGALE
   Ha, ha, ha!
HIERONIMO   Ha, ha, ha!   30
   Why, ha, ha, ha! Farewell, good, ha, ha, ha!
                                            Exit

2 PORTINGALE
   Doubtless this man is passing lunatic,

8–9 lineation ed. (*one line 1592*)
10 *be importunate* insist
18 *baleful humours* evil tendencies, habits of mind
18 *uphold* persist in
21 *hugy* huge, profound
22 *kindled* set on fire   27 *fell* cruel
30–1 lineation ed. (*one line 1592*)
32 *passing* exceedingly

13 Compare I, i, 63–71 and note. Lorenzo is, according to Hieronimo, in
   'the deepest hell'.

Or imperfection of his age doth make him dote.
Come, let's away to seek my lord the duke.

[*Exeunt*]

Act III, Scene xii

Enter HIERONIMO, *with a poniard in one hand, and a rope in the
other*

HIERONIMO

Now sir, perhaps I come and see the king,
The king sees me, and fain would hear my suit:
Why, is not this a strange and seld-seen thing,
That standers-by with toys should strike me mute?
Go to, I see their shifts, and say no more.   5
Hieronimo, 'tis time for thee to trudge:
Down by the dale that flows with purple gore
Standeth a fiery tower; there sits a judge
Upon a seat of steel and molten brass,
And 'twixt his teeth he holds a fire-brand,   10
That leads unto the lake where hell doth stand.
Away, Hieronimo, to him be gone:
He'll do thee justice for Horatio's death.
Turn down this path, thou shalt be with him straight;
Or this, and then thou need'st not take thy breath.   15
This way or that way? Soft and fair, not so:
For if I hang or kill myself, let's know

33 *imperfection of his age* decrepitude, the declining powers of old age
1 s.d. *poniard* dagger
3 *seld* seldom
4 *toys* trifles; trivial business
5 *shifts* tricks
6 *trudge* get moving (*not* slowly)
7 *purple* blood-red
11 *leads* shows the way to
14 *straight* right away
17 *kill* stab

---

1 s.d. Hieronimo carries, as Boas remarks, 'the stock "properties" of a
would-be suicide' in Elizabethan drama.
7 ff. Hieronimo's search for justice takes place in a landscape that directly
recalls Andrea's search for a resting-place in the afterworld (see I, i);
Kyd is anxious to draw out the analogies between the two quests.
14–15 *this path* . . . *Or this* by killing himself with poniard or rope. Schick
points out that ll.14–19 present the same ideas as the last three lines
of the Latin dirge (II, v, 78–80).

Who will revenge Horatio's murder then?
No, no! fie, no! pardon me, I'll none of that:
                He flings away the dagger and halter
This way I'll take, and this way comes the king;   20
                        He takes them up again
And here I'll have a fling at him, that's flat;
And, Balthazar, I'll be with thee to bring,
And thee, Lorenzo! Here's the king; nay, stay,
And here, ay here; there goes the hare away.

            Enter KING, AMBASSADOR, CASTILE, *and* LORENZO
KING
Now show, Ambassador, what our viceroy saith: 25
Hath he received the articles we sent?
HIERONIMO
Justice, O, justice to Hieronimo.
LORENZO
Back, see'st thou not the king is busy?
HIERONIMO
O, is he so?
KING
Who is he that interrupts our business?   30
HIERONIMO
Not I. Hieronimo, beware: go by, go by.
AMBASSADOR
Renowned king, he hath received and read
Thy kingly proffers, and thy promised league,
And, as a man extremely overjoyed
To hear his son so princely entertained,   35
Whose death he had so solemnly bewailed,
This for thy further satisfaction
And kingly love, he kindly lets thee know:
First, for the marriage of his princely son
With Bel-imperia, thy beloved niece,   40
The news are more delightful to his soul,
Than myrrh or incense to the offended heavens.

21 *that's flat* I have made up my mind
22 *I'll . . . bring* I'll get even with you
24 *there . . . away* Edwards explains the phrase refers to losing
    something one has tried to achieve or hold: Hieronimo sees the
    king passing by, preoccupied by business
31 *go by, go by* beware, don't get into trouble

25–30 Hieronimo is thwarted by the day-to-day preoccupations of court
      business; as he foresaw at ll.1–5.

In person, therefore, will be come himself,
To see the marriage rites solemnised;
And, in the presence of the court of Spain,   45
To knit a sure, inexplicable band
Of kingly love, and everlasting league,
Betwixt the crowns of Spain and Portingale,
There will he give his crown to Balthazar,
And make a queen of Bel-imperia.   50

KING
Brother, how like you this our viceroy's love?

CASTILE
No doubt, my lord, it is an argument
Of honourable care to keep his friend,
And wondrous zeal to Balthazar his son;
Nor am I least indebted to his grace,   55
That bends his liking to my daughter thus.

AMBASSADOR
Now last, dread lord, here hath his highness sent
(Although he send not that his son return)
His ransom due to Don Horatio.

HIERONIMO
Horatio! who calls Horatio?   60

KING
And well remembered, thank his majesty.
Here, see it given to Horatio.

HIERONIMO
Justice, O justice, justice, gentle king!

KING
Who is that? Hieronimo?

HIERONIMO
Justice, O, justice! O my son, my son,   65
My son, whom naught can ransom or redeem!

---

46 *inexplicable* ed. (inexecrable *1592*) which cannot be untied
52 *argument* demonstration, proof
56 *bends* directs   58 *that* in order that

---

46 *inexplicable 1594*'s reading, unique in that text for the extent of its
   departure from the earlier edition, is here preferred to *1592*'s 'inexecrable', on grounds of meaning. Edwards points out that *1594* might have
   been set up from a copy of *1592* which contained a corrected forme of
   inner G (and this reading); the sole surviving copy of *1592* would on
   that supposition contain an *uncorrected* inner G.
62 The King alone seems unaware that Horatio is dead; an extremely
   implausible situation.

LORENZO
Hieronimo, you are not well-advised.
HIERONIMO
Away, Lorenzo, hinder me no more,
For thou hast made me bankrupt of my bliss.
Give me my son, you shall not ransom him!   70
Away! I'll rip the bowels of the earth,
                              He diggeth with his dagger
And ferry over to th' Elysian plains,
And bring my son to show his deadly wounds.
Stand from about me!
I'll make a pickaxe of my poniard,   75
And here surrender up my marshalship:
For I'll go marshal up the fiends in hell,
To be avenged on you all for this.
KING
What means this outrage?
Will none of you restrain his fury?   80
HIERONIMO
Nay, soft and fair: you shall not need to strive,
Needs must he go that the devils drive.   *Exit*
KING
What accident hath happed Hieronimo?
I have not seen him to demean him so.
LORENZO
My gracious lord, he is with extreme pride,   85
Conceived of young Horatio his son,
And covetous of having to himself
The ransom of the young prince Balthazar,
Distract, and in a manner lunatic.
KING
Believe me, nephew, we are sorry for't: 90
This is the love that fathers bear their sons.
But, gentle brother, go give to him this gold,
The prince's ransom; let him have his due.
For what he hath Horatio shall not want:
Haply Hieronimo hath need thereof.   95

70 *you . . . him* i.e., from death
72 *th'Elysian plains* see III, viii, 9 and note
74–5 lineation ed. (*one line 1592*)
79 *outrage* violent outburst
79–80 lineation ed. (*one line 1592*)
83 *happed* happened to
84 *demean him* behave himself   95 *Haply* perhaps

LORENZO
> But if he be thus helplessly distract,
> 'Tis requisite his office be resigned,
> And given to one of more discretion.

KING
> We shall increase his melancholy so.
> 'Tis best that we see further in it first;   100
> Till when, ourself will exempt the place.
> And brother, now bring in the ambassador,
> That he may be a witness of the match
> 'Twixt Balthazar and Bel-imperia,
> And that we may prefix a certain time,   105
> Wherein the marriage shall be solemnised,
> That we may have thy lord the viceroy here.

AMBASSADOR
> Therein your highness highly shall content
> His majesty, that longs to hear from hence.

KING
> On, then, and hear you, Lord Ambassador.   *Exeunt* 110

Act III, Scene xiii

Enter HIERONIMO *with a book in his hand*

HIERONIMO
> *Vindicta mihi!*
> Ay, heaven will be revenged of every ill,
> Nor will they suffer murder unrepaid:

100 *see further in it* examine the business further
1 s.p. HIERONIMO ed. (*not in 1592*)

---

101 *ourself will exempt the place* I have retained the 1592 reading despite
difficulties over the meaning of 'exempt' and despite the line's being
one syllable short. The latter difficulty may not be a real one: the line
would *act* perfectly well as it stands. 'Exempt' I take to mean something
like 'hold in suspense': the King will avoid the indignity, for Hieronimo,
of replacing him (Lorenzo's suggestion at ll.96-8), and instead will
continue the crown's judicial functions without an active Knight
Marshal. Collier's emendation, 'execute', is attractive in that it presents
the same idea more explicitly.
1 s.d. Hieronimo carries a copy of Seneca, as later quotations show.
1 *Vindicta mihi* Hieronimo quotes the Biblical admonition 'vengeance is
mine; I will repay, saith the Lord' (Romans xii. 19), a statement much
used by Elizabethan writers to reserve the execution of vengeance to
God. The next four lines expand this attitude.

Then stay, Hieronimo, attend their will,
For mortal men may not appoint their time.   5
'Per scelus semper tutum est sceleribus iter.'
Strike, and strike home, where wrong is offered thee;
For evils unto ills conductors be,
And death's the worst of resolution.
For he that thinks with patience to contend   10
To quiet life, his life shall easily end.
'Fata si miseros juvant, habes salutem;
Fata si vitam negant, habes sepulchrum.'
If destiny thy miseries do ease,
Then hast thou health, and happy shalt thou be;   15
If destiny deny thee life, Hieronimo,
Yet shalt thou be assured of a tomb;
If neither, yet let this thy comfort be,
Heaven covereth him that hath no burial.
And to conclude, I will revenge his death!   20
But how? not as the vulgar wits of men,
With open, but inevitable ills,
As by a secret, yet a certain mean,
Which under kindship will be cloaked best.

4 *attend their will* await Heaven's pleasure
9 *death's . . . resolution* death is the worst that can follow bold
conduct
10 *contend* strive, make one's way
21 *vulgar* common
22 *inevitable* inevitably successful   22 *ills* ill practices
23 *mean* course of action
24 *kindship* kindness   24 *cloaked* hidden

6 'The safe way for crimes is through (further) crimes'. Hieronimo reads
from the Seneca he holds in his hand (the Latin is an adaptation of
Seneca's *Agamemnon*, l.115). Prompted by the Senecan tag, he reflects
that Lorenzo will probably try to secure his own safety by adding a
crime against himself to the crime against Horatio (see ll.10–11).
It is this reflection that prompts his abandoning the argument for
Christian patience of the first five lines.
12–13 Again Hieronimo reads from Seneca (here *Troades*, ll.511–12).
The next four lines give a loose translation.
18 *neither* Presumably Hieronimo means neither health nor tomb.
22–3 rather clumsily expressed. Hieronimo means perhaps that simple-
minded men ('vulgar wits') seek vengeance by methods which are bold
and obvious ('open'), yet despite this effective; he, however, will use
subtlety, though the subtlety will not endanger his plan's effectiveness.
The main contrast is between crude force and the witty devices Hieronimo is considering.

Wise men will take their opportunity,   25
Closely and safely fitting things to time.
But in extremes advantage hath no time;
And therefore all times fit not for revenge.
Thus therefore will I rest me in unrest,
Dissembling quiet in unquietness,   30
Not seeming that I know their villainies;
That my simplicity may make them think
That ignorantly I will let all slip—
For ignorance, I wot, and well they know,
Remedium malorum iners est.   35
Nor aught avails it me to menace them,
Who, as a wintry storm upon a plain,
Will bear me down with their nobility.
No, no, Hieronimo, thou must enjoin
Thine eyes to observation, and thy tongue   40
To milder speeches than thy spirit affords,
Thy heart to patience, and thy hands to rest,
Thy cap to courtesy, and thy knee to bow,
Till to revenge thou know, when, where and how.
                              A noise within
How now, what noise? what coil is that you keep?   45

Enter a SERVANT

SERVANT
Here are a sort of poor petitioners,
That are importunate, and it shall please you, sir,
That you should plead their cases to the king.

---

26 *Closely* with subtlety   26 *time* opportunity
32 *simplicity* apparently undesigning behaviour
38 *nobility* noble rank   44 s.d. *follows l.45 in 1592*
45 *what coil . . . keep?* what is all that noise you are making?
46 *sort* group, company   47 *and* if

27–8 'But' here means 'only'; Hieronimo says that only crises ('extremes')
    exclude the possibility of waiting for a favourable moment ('advantage');
    revenge, being considered and deliberate, requires that one waits one's
    opportunity.
29–33 Hieronimo's proposed stealth need not conflict with his sense that
    Heaven prompts and supports him (see e.g. IV, i, 32–4 and III, vii,
    45–56). Johnson (p. 29) quotes Calvin's remark that in dealing with the
    wicked 'God shewed himself a revenger by little and little, and as
    it were faire and softly' (i.e. stealthily).
35 'is an unskilful antidote to evils.' A further quotation from Seneca
    (adapted from *Oedipus* l.515) but not, I think, read from the book.

HIERONIMO
  That I should plead their several actions?
  Why, let them enter, and let me see them.   50

          Enter three CITIZENS *and an* OLD MAN
1 CITIZEN
  So, I tell you this, for learning and for law,
  There's not any advocate in Spain
  That can prevail, or will take half the pain
  That he will, in pursuit of equity.
HIERONIMO
  Come near, you men, that thus importune me.   55
  [*Aside*] Now must I bear a face of gravity,
  For thus I used, before my marshalship,
  To plead in causes as corregidor.—
  Come on sirs, what's the matter?
2 CITIZEN   Sir, an action.
HIERONIMO
  Of battery?
1 CITIZEN   Mine of debt.
HIERONIMO   Give place.   60
2 CITIZEN
  No sir, mine is an action of the case.
3 CITIZEN
  Mine an *ejectione firmae* by a lease.
HIERONIMO
  Content you sirs, are you determined
  That I should plead your several actions?
1 CITIZEN
  Ay sir, and here's my declaration.   65
2 CITIZEN
  And here is my band.

49 *actions* cases in law
58 *corregidor* advocate. Strictly, Edwards notes, the chief magistrate
   of a Spanish town
61 *action of the case* An action not within the limited jurisdiction
   of the Common Pleas needed a special writ to cover it. These
   special writs were known as 'actions of trespass on the case' or
   'actions on the case' (Edwards)
62 *ejectione firmae* 'a writ to eject a tenant from his holding before
   the expiration of his lease' (Edwards). Kyd's 'by a lease' is
   difficult to account for
62 *firmae* ed. (firma *1592*)
65 *declaration* in law, the plaintiff's statement of claim
66 *band* bond; the special writ referred to at l.61 and note

3 CITIZEN   And here is my lease.
                                    They give him papers
HIERONIMO
    But wherefore stands yon silly man so mute,
    With mournful eyes and hands to heaven upreared?
    Come hither, father, let me know thy cause.
SENEX
    O worthy sir, my cause, but slightly known,   70
    May move the hearts of warlike Myrmidons
    And melt the Corsic rocks with ruthful tears.
HIERONIMO
    Say, father, tell me what's thy suit?
SENEX
    No sir, could my woes
    Give way unto my most distressful words,   75
    Then should I not in paper, as you see,
    With ink bewray what blood began in me.
HIERONIMO
    What's here? 'The humble supplication
    Of Don Bazulto for his murdered son.'
SENEX
    Ay sir.
HIERONIMO No sir, it was my murdered son,   80
    O my son, my son, O my son Horatio!
    But mine, or thine, Bazulto, be content.
    Here, take my handkercher, and wipe thine eyes,
    Whiles wretched I in thy mishaps may see
    The lively portrait of my dying self.   85
                            He draweth out a bloody napkin
    O no, not this: Horatio, this was thine,
    And when I dyed it in thy dearest blood,

67 *silly* simple, pitiable
71 *Myrmidons* Achilles' followers; a Thessalian tribe noted for their
    fierceness
72 *Corsic* of Corsica; Seneca's *Octavia* (II.i. in Newton's ed., 1581)
    has a reference to the 'craggy corsicke rockes' among which
    Seneca lived in exile
77 *blood* passion
80-1 lineation ed. (my murdred sonne, oh my sonne. / My sonne . . .
    Horatio. 1592)
85 *lively* living

78-9 Shakespeare uses similar parallels (of sons who have lost fathers)
    in *Hamlet*. Hieronimo's shame (see ll.95 ff.) parallels Hamlet's after
    watching the First Player act the tale of Priam.

This was a token 'twixt thy soul and me
That of thy death revenged I should be.
But here, take this, and this—what, my purse?—   90
Ay, this, and that, and all of them are thine;
For all as one are our extremities.

1 CITIZEN
O see the kindness of Hieronimo!

2 CITIZEN
This gentleness shows him a gentleman.

HIERONIMO
See, see, O see thy shame, Hieronimo,   95
See here a loving father to his son!
Behold the sorrows and the sad laments
That he delivereth for his son's decease!
If love's effects so strives in lesser things,
If love enforce such moods in meaner wits,   100
If love express such power in poor estates—
Hieronimo, whenas a raging sea
Tossed with the wind and tide, o'erturneth then
The upper billows, course of waves to keep,
Whilst lesser waters labour in the deep,   105
Then sham'st thou not, Hieronimo, to neglect
The sweet revenge of thy Horatio?
Though on this earth justice will not be found,
I'll down to hell, and in this passion
Knock at the dismal gates of Pluto's court,   110
Getting by force, as once Alcides did,

90 *this* this coin   92 *extremities* extreme sufferings
100 *meaner* of lower social rank
102 *whenas* ed. (when as *1592*)
103 *o'erturneth* ed. (ore turnest *1592*)
109 *passion* suffering, deep emotion
110 *Pluto* god of the underworld
111 *Alcides* Heracles or Hercules, who in his twelfth labour descended
    to the underworld and conquered Cerberus

102–7 A difficult passage to explain. Hieronimo may mean that in storm
    conditions (i.e. in a time of grief) the surface of the sea is driven into
    great waves (the response of the 'upper waters' to the grief-storm),
    while other and less majestic waters ('lesser waters') are troubled too.
    I think Hieronimo sees himself as, in social standing, equivalent to the
    'upper billows' and is ashamed he has not kept his 'course of waves';
    the Old Man has responded as lesser waters should. (For an alternative
    explanation, reversing the roles, see Edwards.) 'In the deep' need not
    mean 'in the depths' but merely 'in the sea'.

A troop of Furies and tormenting hags
To torture Don Lorenzo and the rest.
Yet lest the triple-headed porter should
Deny my passage to the slimy strond,　　　　　　　　115
The Thracian poet thou shalt counterfeit:
Come on, old father, be my Orpheus,
And if thou canst no notes upon the harp,
Then sound the burden of thy sore heart's grief,
Till we do gain that Proserpine may grant　　　　　120
Revenge on them that murdered my son.
Then will I rent and tear them thus and thus,
Shivering their limbs in pieces with my teeth.

Tear the papers

1 CITIZEN
O sir, my declaration!

Exit HIERONIMO *and they after*

2 CITIZEN
Save my bond!　　　　　　　　　　　　　　　125

Enter HIERONIMO

2 CITIZEN
Save my bond!
3 CITIZEN
Alas, my lease! it cost me ten pound,
And you, my lord, have torn the same.
HIERONIMO
That cannot be, I gave it never a wound;
Show me one drop of blood fall from the same:　　　130
How is it possible I should slay it then?
Tush, no; run after, catch me if you can.

Exeunt all but the OLD MAN

114 *triple-headed porter* the three-headed monstrous dog Cerberus,
　　guardian of the underworld　　　　115 *slimy strond* see I, i, 27–9
116 *Thracian poet* Orpheus (see next note)
117 *Orpheus* the legendary poet and master of music who followed his
　　dead wife Eurydice to the underworld and induced Persephone
　　(Proserpine) by his playing to let her go (see following lines)
119 *burden* the theme or refrain of a song　　　122 *rent* rend

120–1 The audience knows that Proserpine has already granted his request
　　(I, i, 78 ff.).
132 The similarity to Hamlet's behaviour after the killing of Polonius is
　　striking (*Hamlet*, IV, ii). Hieronimo's mistaking the Old Man in the
　　following lines is perhaps more acceptable to modern taste, as a way of
　　expressing obsession, than Hamlet's vision of the Ghost in the Closet
　　scene.

BAZULTO *remains till* HIERONIMO *enters again, who, staring him in the face, speaks*

HIERONIMO
    And art thou come, Horatio, from the depth,
    To ask for justice in this upper earth?
    To tell thy father thou art unrevenged,   135
    To wring more tears from Isabella's eyes,
    Whose lights are dimmed with over-long laments?
    Go back my son, complain to Aeacus,
    For here's no justice; gentle boy be gone,
    For justice is exiled from the earth;   140
    Hieronimo will bear thee company.
    Thy mother cries on righteous Rhadamanth
    For just revenge against the murderers.
SENEX
    Alas my lord, whence springs this troubled speech?
HIERONIMO
    But let me look on my Horatio.   145
    Sweet boy, how art thou changed in death's black shade!
    Had Proserpine no pity on thy youth,
    But suffered thy fair crimson-coloured spring
    With withered winter to be blasted thus?
    Horatio, thou art older than thy father;   150
    Ah ruthless fate, that favour thus transforms!
SENEX
    Ah my good lord, I am not your young son.
HIERONIMO
    What, not my son? thou, then, a Fury art,
    Sent from the empty kingdom of black night
    To summon me to make appearance   155
    Before grim Minos and just Rhadamanth,
    To plague Hieronimo that is remiss,
    And seeks not vengeance for Horatio's death.

137 *lights* eyes
138 *Aeacus* a judge of the underworld; see I, i, 33
142 *cries on* pleads to
142 *Rhadamanth* a judge of the underworld; see I, i, 33
149 *blasted* blighted
151 *fate* ed. (Father *1592*)
151 *favour* appearance, looks
153 *Fury* avenging spirit
156 *Minos* the third judge of the underworld; 'grim' appears to
    contradict the estimate of Minos given at I, i, 50

SENEX
    I am a grieved man, and not a ghost,
    That came for justice for my murdered son.   160
HIERONIMO
    Ay, now I know thee, now thou nam'st thy son;
    Thou art the lively image of my grief:
    Within thy face my sorrows I may see.
    Thy eyes are gummed with tears, thy cheeks are wan,
    Thy forehead troubled, and thy muttering lips   165
    Murmur sad words abruptly broken off
    By force of windy sighs thy spirit breathes;
    And all this sorrow riseth for thy son:
    And selfsame sorrow feel I for my son.
    Come in old man, thou shalt to Isabel;   170
    Lean on my arm: I thee, thou me shalt stay,
    And thou, and I, and she, will sing a song,
    Three parts in one, but all of discords framed—
    Talk not of cords, but let us now be gone,
    For with a cord Horatio was slain.   *Exeunt* 175

Act III, Scene xiv

Enter KING *of* SPAIN, *the* DUKE, VICEROY, *and* LORENZO,
    BALTHAZAR, DON PEDRO, *and* BEL-IMPERIA

KING
    Go brother, it is the Duke of Castile's cause,
    Salute the viceroy in our name.
CASTILE   I go.
VICEROY
    Go forth, Don Pedro, for thy nephew's sake,
    And greet the Duke of Castile.
PEDRO   It shall be so.
KING
    And now to meet these Portuguese,   5
    For as we now are, so sometimes were these,

161 *thy* ed. (my *1592*)
162 *lively* living
171 *stay* sustain, prop up
174 *cords* punning on the musical 'chord' and cord meaning rope
1–2 lineation ed. (*as prose 1592*)

6–7 Freeman (pp. 53–4) says that 'western Indies' here refers to Portuguese Brazil, a prize taken by Spain during the quarrels with Portugal of
the late sixteenth century.

Kings and commanders of the western Indies.
Welcome, brave viceroy, to the court of Spain,
And welcome all his honourable train.
'Tis not unknown to us, for why you come,   10
Or have so kingly crossed the seas:
Sufficeth it, in this we note the troth
And more than common love you lend to us.
So is it that mine honourable niece,
(For it beseems us now that it be known)   15
Already is betrothed to Balthazar,
And by appointment and our condescent
To-morrow are they to be married.
To this intent we entertain thyself,
Thy followers, their pleasure and our peace.   20
Speak, men of Portingale, shall it be so?
If ay, say so; if not, say flatly no.

VICEROY

Renowned king, I come not as thou think'st,
With doubtful followers, unresolved men,
But such as have upon thine articles   25
Confirmed thy motion and contented me.
Know sovereign, I come to solemnise
The marriage of thy beloved niece,
Fair Bel-imperia, with my Balthazar—
With thee, my son; whom sith I live to see,   30
Here take my crown, I give it her and thee;
And let me live a solitary life,
In ceaseless prayers,
To think how strangely heaven hath thee preserved.

KING

See brother, see, how nature strives in him!   35
Come, worthy viceroy, and accompany

 9 *train* company, followers
12 *troth* loyalty
17 *condescent* agreement
20 *their* i.e. Bel-imperia and Balthazar   26 *motion* proposal
34 *strangely* wonderfully
35 *nature strives in him* he weeps

11 This looks like an absurd error, though Freeman (p. 12) suggests that
   the play may be set in Seville, frequently the seat of the Spanish court;
   in this case a Portuguese deputation might well travel partly by sea
   (via Cadiz).

Thy friend with thine extremities;
A place more private fits this princely mood.
VICEROY
Or here or where your highness thinks it good.
                    Exeunt all but CASTILE *and* LORENZO
CASTILE
Nay stay, Lorenzo, let me talk with you.   40
See'st thou this entertainment of these kings?
LORENZO
I do, my lord, and joy to see the same.
CASTILE
And knowest thou why this meeting is?
LORENZO
For her, my lord, whom Balthazar doth love,
And to confirm their promised marriage.   45
CASTILE
She is thy sister?
LORENZO   Who, Bel-imperia?
Ay, my gracious lord, and this is the day
That I have longed so happily to see.
CASTILE
Thou wouldst be loath that any fault of thine
Should intercept her in her happiness.   50
LORENZO
Heavens will not let Lorenzo err so much.
CASTILE
Why then, Lorenzo, listen to my words:
It is suspected and reported too,
That thou, Lorenzo, wrong'st Hieronimo,
And in his suits towards his majesty   55
Still keep'st him back, and seeks to cross his suit.
LORENZO
That I, my lord—?
CASTILE
I tell thee son, myself have heard it said,
When, to my sorrow, I have been ashamed
To answer for thee, though thou art my son.   60
Lorenzo, knowest thou not the common love

37 *extremities* extreme emotions
41 *entertainment* greeting, hospitable reception
46–8 lineation ed. (She ... Sister? / Who ... Lord, / And ... see.
    1592)
50 *intercept* obstruct
56 *cross* interrupt, prevent   61 *common* widespread

And kindness that Hieronimo hath won
By his deserts within the court of Spain?
Or seest thou not the king my brother's care
In his behalf, and to procure his health?   65
Lorenzo, shouldst thou thwart his passions,
And he exclaim against thee to the king,
What honour were't in this assembly,
Or what a scandal were't among the kings
To hear Hieronimo exclaim on thee?   70
Tell me, and look thou tell me truly too,
Whence grows the ground of this report in court?

LORENZO
My lord, it lies not in Lorenzo's power
To stop the vulgar, liberal of their tongues:
A small advantage makes a water-breach,   75
And no man lives that long contenteth all.

CASTILE
Myself have seen thee busy to keep back
Him and his supplications from the king.

LORENZO
Yourself, my lord, hath seen his passions,
That ill beseemed the presence of a king;   80
And for I pitied him in his distress,
I held him thence with kind and courteous words,
As free from malice to Hieronimo
As to my soul, my lord.

CASTILE
Hieronimo, my son, mistakes thee then.   85

LORENZO
My gracious father, believe me so he doth.
But what's a silly man, distract in mind,
To think upon the murder of his son?
Alas, how easy is it for him to err!
But for his satisfaction and the world's,   90
'Twere good, my lord, that Hieronimo and I
Were reconciled, if he misconster me.

66 *passions* laments, complaints
67 *exclaim against* denounce
74 *vulgar, liberal* ed. (vulgar liberall *1592*) common people, free with
75 *advantage* opportunity (for exploitation), weakness
75 *water-breach* a gap in wall or dyke caused by water-pressure
80 *ill beseemed* fitted ill with
87 *silly* simple, poor
92 *misconster* misconstrue, wilfully misinterpret

CASTILE
 Lorenzo, thou hast said; it shall be so;
 Go one of you and call Hieronimo.

                Enter BALTHAZAR *and* BEL-IMPERIA

BALTHAZAR
 Come, Bel-imperia, Balthazar's content,   95
 My sorrow's ease and sovereign of my bliss,
 Sith heaven hath ordained thee to be mine;
 Disperse those clouds and melancholy looks,
 And clear them up with those thy sun-bright eyes,
 Wherein my hope and heaven's fair beauty lies.   100
BEL-IMPERIA
 My looks, my lord, are fitting for my love,
 Which new begun, can show no brighter yet.
BALTHAZAR
 New kindled flames should burn as morning sun.
BEL-IMPERIA
 But not too fast, lest heat and all be done.
 I see my lord my father.
BALTHAZAR   Truce, my love;   105
 I will go salute him.
CASTILE   Welcome, Balthazar,
 Welcome brave prince, the pledge of Castile's peace;
 And welcome Bel-imperia. How now, girl?
 Why com'st thou sadly to salute us thus?
 Content thyself, for I am satisfied;   110
 It is not now as when Andrea lived,
 We have forgotten and forgiven that,
 And thou art graced with a happier love.
 But Balthazar, here comes Hieronimo,
 I'll have a word with him.   115

---

102 *no brighter* ed. (brighter *1592*)
105–7 lineation ed. (I see . . . Father. / Truce . . . him. / Welcome . .
    Prince, / The . . . peace: *1592*)
109 *sadly* with serious looks

---

102 *no brighter 1594*'s emendation (*1592* omits 'no') must be right; *1592*
    makes sense ('there's time for them to get brighter') but asks Bel-
    imperia to be coyly encouraging, an improbable attitude here.
110–13 yet another reference to the disapproval felt for Bel-imperia's
    liaison with Andrea (see I, i, 10–11 and note).

Enter HIERONIMO *and a* SERVANT

HIERONIMO
  And where's the duke?
SERVANT   Yonder.
HIERONIMO   Even so:
  What new device have they devised, trow?
  Pocas palabras! mild as the lamb,
  Is't I will be revenged? No, I am not the man.
CASTILE
  Welcome Hieronimo.   120
LORENZO
  Welcome Hieronimo.
BALTHAZAR
  Welcome Hieronimo.
HIERONIMO
  My lords, I thank you for Horatio.
CASTILE
  Hieronimo, the reason that I sent
  To speak with you, is this.
HIERONIMO   What, so short?   125
  Then I'll be gone, I thank you for't.
CASTILE
  Nay, stay, Hieronimo—go call him, son.
LORENZO
  Hieronimo, my father craves a word with you.
HIERONIMO
  With me sir? why, my lord, I thought you had done.
LORENZO
  [Aside] No, would he had.
CASTILE   Hieronimo, I hear   130
  You find yourself aggrieved at my son
  Because you have not access unto the king,
  And say 'tis he that intercepts your suits.

116–17 lineation ed. (*one line 1592*)
117 *device* plot
117 *trow?* do you think?
118 *Pocas palabras* few words (Spanish)
128 s.p. LORENZO ed. (*not in 1592*)
130–1 lineation ed. (No, . . . had. / Hieronimo . . . Sonne, *1592*)
133 *intercepts* obstructs, thwarts

117–19 Hieronimo now feels threatened, like Hamlet later, by plots ('devices') on all sides.

HIERONIMO
Why, is not this a miserable thing, my lord?
CASTILE
Hieronimo, I hope you have no cause,   135
And would be loath that one of your deserts
Should once have reason to suspect my son,
Considering how I think of you myself.
HIERONIMO
Your son Lorenzo! whom, my noble lord?
The hope of Spain, mine honourable friend?   140
Grant me the combat of them, if they dare:
                                   Draws out his sword
I'll meet him face to face, to tell me so.
These be the scandalous reports of such
As love not me, and hate my lord too much.
Should I suspect Lorenzo would prevent   145
Or cross my suit, that loved my son so well?
My lord, I am ashamed it should be said.
LORENZO
Hieronimo, I never gave you cause.
HIERONIMO
My good lord, I know you did not.
CASTILE   There then pause,
And for the satisfaction of the world,   150
Hieronimo, frequent my homely house,
The Duke of Castile, Cyprian's ancient seat,
And when thou wilt, use me, my son, and it.
But here, before Prince Balthazar and me,
Embrace each other, and be perfect friends.   155
HIERONIMO
Ay marry, my lord, and shall.
Friends, quoth he? see, I'll be friends with you all:
Specially with you, my lovely lord;
For divers causes it is fit for us
That we be friends—the world is suspicious,   160
And men may think what we imagine not.

141 *the combat of them* the right to meet them in (hand-to-hand)
     combat
144 *love* ed. (loues *1592*)
145 *prevent* forestall, obstruct
146 *cross* thwart
149–50 lineation ed. (There . . . world *one line 1592*)
151 *homely* welcoming, hospitable, 'home-like'
153 *use* make use of, ask the services of

BALTHAZAR
Why, this is friendly done, Hieronimo.
LORENZO
And thus I hope old grudges are forgot.
HIERONIMO
What else? it were a shame it should not be so.
CASTILE
Come on, Hieronimo, at my request;   165
Let us intreat your company today.
                        Exeunt [all but HIERONIMO]
HIERONIMO
Your lordship's to command.—Pha! keep your way:
Chi mi fa più carezze che non suole,
Tradito mi ha, o tradir vuole.   *Exit*

Act III, Scene xv

Ghost [of ANDREA] *and* REVENGE

ANDREA
Awake, Erichtho! Cerberus, awake!
Solicit Pluto, gentle Proserpine;
To combat, Acheron and Erebus!
For ne'er by Styx and Phlegethon in hell
. . . .   5
Nor ferried Charon to the fiery lakes

163 *thus* ed. (that *1592*)
167 *Pha!* an exclamation of contempt or disgust
168 *Chi . . . suole* ed. (*Mi. Chi mi fa? Pui Correzza Che non sule 1592*)
169 *Tradito . . . vuole* ed. (*Tradito viha otrade vule. 1592*)
1 s.d. Ghost ed. (Enter *Ghoast 1592*)
1 s.p. ANDREA ed. (*Ghost 1592 throughout this scene*)
1 *Erichtho* ed. (*Erictha 1592*) 'the Thessalian sorceress' (Schick)
3 *Acheron* ed. (*Achinon 1592*) see III, i, 55 and note
3 *Erebus* ed. (*Ericus 1592*) primaeval darkness, child of chaos
4 *ne'er* ed. (neere *1592*)
4 *Styx and Phlegethon* rivers of the underworld
4 *in hell* (*end of l.3 in 1592*)   6 *Charon* see I, i, 20 and note at I, i, 19

168–9 'He who gives me more caresses than usual has betrayed me or
    wishes to betray me.'
4–7 I accept Edwards's supposition that a line has dropped out after l.4
    (he suggests it might have been something like 'Was I distressed with
    outrage sore as this'). Only on this basis can the passage be made to
    give reasonable sense.

Such fearful sights, as poor Andrea sees!
Revenge, awake!

REVENGE

Awake? for why?

ANDREA

Awake, Revenge, for thou art ill-advised   10
To sleep away what thou art warned to watch!

REVENGE

Content thyself, and do not trouble me.

ANDREA

Awake, Revenge, if love, as love hath had,
Have yet the power or prevalence in hell!
Hieronimo with Lorenzo is joined in league,   15
And intercepts our passage to revenge:
Awake, Revenge, or we are woe-begone!

REVENGE

Thus worldlings ground, what they have dreamed, upon.
Content thyself, Andrea: though I sleep,
Yet is my mood soliciting their souls;   20
Sufficeth thee that poor Hieronimo
Cannot forget his son Horatio.
Nor dies Revenge although he sleep awhile,

7 *sees!* ed. (see? *1592*)
11 *To sleep* ed. (Thsleep *1592*)
11 away ed. (away, *1592*)
11 *sleep away* sleep out
11 *watch* stay awake
14 *prevalence* ed. (preuailance *1592*)
17 *begone* ed. (degone *1592*)
20 *mood* Edwards thinks 'anger' just possible; a more general sense
    such as 'attitude', 'purposes' seems required

8 ff. The repetitions of 'Awake' may seem crude, and there is considerable
    suspicion that the text of this scene as a whole is a debased one (see
    Edwards, esp. pp. xxxiii and xxxviii–xxxix), yet the action does have
    dramatic point in giving emphatic expression to Andrea's sense that
    vengeance is becoming less and less probable — even Hieronimo seems
    to have betrayed the cause (see l.15). Elizabethans would have under-
    stood the scene as referring to the 'worldling's' (see l.18) faithless
    supposition that delay is equivalent to the abandoning of God's (or
    Revenge's) purposes.
11 *away* Edwards may be correct in accepting Hawkins's emendation
    'awake!' in place of *1592*'s 'away'; but the text makes good sense as it
    stands and I see no compelling grounds for emendation.
18 *worldlings . . . upon* 'mortals base their beliefs on what they have merely
    dreamed (or fancied)'.

For in unquiet, quietness is feigned,
And slumbering is a common worldly wile.   25
Behold, Andrea, for an instance how
Revenge hath slept, and then imagine thou
What 'tis to be subject to destiny.

Enter a Dumb Show [; they act and exeunt]

ANDREA
Awake, Revenge, reveal this mystery.
REVENGE
The two first, the nuptial torches bore,   30
As brightly burning as the mid-day's sun;
But after them doth Hymen hie as fast,
Clothed in sable, and a saffron robe,
And blows them out, and quencheth them with blood,
As discontent that things continue so.   35
ANDREA
Sufficeth me; thy meaning's understood;
And thanks to thee and those infernal powers
That will not tolerate a lover's woe.
Rest thee, for I will sit to see the rest.
REVENGE
Then argue not, for thou hast thy request.   40

Exeunt

Act IV, Scene i

Enter BEL-IMPERIA *and* HIERONIMO

BEL-IMPERIA
Is this the love thou bear'st Horatio?
Is this the kindness that thou counterfeits?
Are these the fruits of thine incessant tears?
Hieronimo, are these thy passions,
Thy protestations and thy deep laments,   5
That thou wert wont to weary men withal?
O unkind father, O deceitful world!

29 *reveal this mystery* explain the secret meaning of this action (the dumb show)
32 *Hymen* god of marriage
32 *hie* run
33 *sable* black
33 *saffron* yellow, the usual colour of Hymen's robe
4 *passions* passionate exclamations
7 *unkind* unnatural

With what excuses canst thou show thyself,
With what..............................
From this dishonour and the hate of men?—   10
Thus to neglect the loss and life of him
Whom both my letters and thine own belief
Assures thee to be causeless slaughtered.
Hieronimo, for shame, Hieronimo,
Be not a history to after times   15
Of such ingratitude unto thy son.
Unhappy mothers of such children then—
But monstrous fathers, to forget so soon
The death of those, whom they with care and cost
Have tendered so, thus careless should be lost.   20
Myself a stranger in respect of thee,
So loved his life, as still I wish their deaths;
Nor shall his death be unrevenged by me,
Although I bear it out for fashion's sake:
For here I swear in sight of heaven and earth,   25
Shouldst thou neglect the love thou shouldst retain
And give it over and devise no more,
Myself should send their hateful souls to hell,
That wrought his downfall with extremest death.

HIERONIMO

But may it be that Bel-imperia   30
Vows such revenge as she hath deigned to say?
Why then, I see that heaven applies our drift

---

9 *With what* . . . ed. (With what dishonour, and the hate of men
   1592)
15 *history* example, tale   20 *tendered* cared for, cherished
21 *in respect of* compared to
24 *bear it* . . . *sake* 'make a pretence of accepting the situation for the
   sake of appearances' (Edwards)
27 *devise* plot   29 *extremest* most cruel
32 *applies our drift* blesses our enterprise (drift, 'what we are
   driving at')

---

9 The dots represent material presumed lost when the *1592* compositor
   inadvertently included in l.9 the last six words of l.10 (see textual
   gloss above). The first two words (as printed) may be either the correct
   first words of the (now missing) l.9 or a mistaken repeat of the beginning
   of l.8. Bungling of some kind has certainly taken place, and since the
   true original cannot be recovered it seems best to indicate this by
   inserting dots.
17–20 an incomplete sentence; just plausible dramatically as reflecting in
   its lack of grammatical structure Bel-imperia's unsettled state of mind.

And all the saints do sit soliciting
For vengeance on those cursed murderers.
Madam 'tis true, and now I find it so;   35
I found a letter, written in your name,
And in that letter, how Horatio died.
Pardon, O pardon, Bel-imperia,
My fear and care in not believing it,
Nor think I thoughtless think upon a mean   40
To let his death be unrevenged at full;
And here I vow, so you but give consent,
And will conceal my resolution,
I will ere long determine of their deaths
That causeless thus have murdered my son.   45

BEL-IMPERIA
Hieronimo, I will consent, conceal;
And aught that may effect for thine avail
Join with thee to revenge Horatio's death.

HIERONIMO
On then; whatsoever I devise,
Let me entreat you, grace my practices.   50
For why, the plot's already in mine head.
Here they are.

Enter BALTHAZAR *and* LORENZO

BALTHAZAR   How now, Hieronimo?
What, courting Bel-imperia?

HIERONIMO   Ay, my lord,
Such courting as, I promise you,
She hath my heart, but you, my lord, have hers.   55

LORENZO
But now, Hieronimo, or never,
We are to entreat your help.

39 *care* caution
40 *thoughtless* unconcerned
44 *determine of* bring about
47 *avail* assistance
50 *grace* support, involve yourself in
51 *For why* because
52–61 lineation ed. (Heere . . . are. / How . . . *Bel-Imperia.* / I . . . you
   / She . . . hers. / But . . . helpe. / My . . . me. / For . . . you. / It . . .
   Embassadour. *1592*)

52 ff. Kyd here allows his actors an excellent opportunity for expressing,
through hypocritical politeness, the tensions between the three men.

HIERONIMO   My help?
  Why, my good lords, assure yourselves of me,
  For you have given me cause,
  Ay, by my faith have you.
BALTHAZAR   It pleased you   60
  At the entertainment of the ambassador
  To grace the king so much as with a show:
  Now were your study so well furnished,
  As, for the passing of the first night's sport,
  To entertain my father with the like,   65
  Or any such-like pleasing motion,
  Assure yourself it would content them well.
HIERONIMO
  Is this all?
BALTHAZAR
  Ay, this is all.
HIERONIMO
  Why then I'll fit you; say no more.   70
  When I was young I gave my mind
  And plied myself to fruitless poetry:
  Which though it profit the professor naught,
  Yet is it passing pleasing to the world.
LORENZO
  And how for that?
HIERONIMO   Marry, my good lord, thus—   75
  And yet, methinks, you are too quick with us—
  When in Toledo there I studied,
  It was my chance to write a tragedy—
  See here my lords—   *He shows them a book*
  Which long forgot, I found this other day.   80
  Now would your lordships favour me so much
  As but to grace me with your acting it—
  I mean each one of you to play a part—

62 *grace* honour
63 *furnished* stocked
66 *motion* entertainment
70 *I'll fit you* (a) 'I'll provide you what you need' (b) 'I'll pay you
   out' or 'I'll punish you as you deserve' (Edwards)
73 *professor* the man who 'professes' or practises it
76 *too quick* too pressing; perhaps with a pun on quick meaning alive

76 unclear. Perhaps the line is meant to convey that Hieronimo's anger
   is only just under control.

Assure you it will prove most passing strange
And wondrous plausible to that assembly.   85
BALTHAZAR
What, would you have us play a tragedy?
HIERONIMO
Why, Nero thought it no disparagement,
And kings and emperors have ta'en delight
To make experience of their wits in plays!
LORENZO
Nay, be not angry good Hieronimo,   90
The prince but asked a question.
BALTHAZAR
In faith, Hieronimo, and you be in earnest,
I'll make one.
LORENZO
And I another.
HIERONIMO
Now my good lord, could you entreat   95
Your sister Bel-imperia to make one?
For what's a play without a woman in it?
BEL-IMPERIA
Little entreaty shall serve me, Hieronimo,
For I must needs be employed in your play.
HIERONIMO
Why, this is well; I tell you lordings,   100
It was determined to have been acted
By gentlemen and scholars too
Such as could tell what to speak.

84 *strange* remarkable, wonderful
85 *plausible* agreeable
87 *disparagement* loss of dignity
89 *experience* trial   92 *and* if
101 *determined* intended, arranged
103 *could tell* knew, were skilful

87 *Nero* Hieronimo is correct in indicating that the Roman emperor Nero
patronised plays and acted in them himself; at the same time he was
associated with violence and deeds of blood, and the audience would no
doubt pick up the allusion. Balthazar's nervousness (l.155) is fully
justified.
103-5 *what to speak . . . how to speak* not clear. Balthazar may mean only
that courtiers are as skilled as 'gentlemen and scholars' in these matters.
Some contrast may be intended between scholars who are good at
invention and courtiers who are good at elocution.

BALTHAZAR
  And now it shall be played by princes and courtiers,
  Such as can tell how to speak,   105
  If, as it is our country manner,
  You will but let us know the argument.
HIERONIMO
  That shall I roundly. The chronicles of Spain
  Record this written of a knight of Rhodes:
  He was betrothed, and wedded at the length   110
  To one Perseda, an Italian dame,
  Whose beauty ravished all that her beheld,
  Especially the soul of Soliman,
  Who at the marriage was the chiefest guest.
  By sundry means sought Soliman to win   115
  Perseda's love, and could not gain the same.
  Then gan he break his passions to a friend,
  One of his bashaws whom he held full dear;
  Her had this bashaw long solicited,
  And saw she was not otherwise to be won   120
  But by her husband's death, this knight of Rhodes,
  Whom presently by treachery he slew.
  She, stirred with an exceeding hate therefore,
  As cause of this slew Soliman;
  And to escape the bashaw's tyranny   125
  Did stab herself: and this the tragedy.
LORENZO
  O excellent!
BEL-IMPERIA   But say, Hieronimo,
  What then became of him that was the bashaw?

---

107 *argument* plot, narrative   108 *roundly* plainly; at once
114 *was* ed. (way *1592*)   117 *break* disclose, confess
118 *bashaws* pashas, Turkish officers of high rank; courtiers
127–8 lineation ed. (O excellent. / But . . . him/That . . . Bashaw? *1592*)

---

107 *let us know the argument* Apparently we should think of the play as
    unscripted: Hieronimo will sketch in the plot and on that basis the
    actors will improvise their own lines. Kyd avoids repeating the 'argu-
    ment' (or plot) by providing the King with a written copy (IV, iii,
    6–7; IV, iv, 9–10). The 'abstracts' referred to at l. 141 would perhaps
    outline the play's narrative a little more fully.
108–40 The playlet of Soliman and Perseda, as well as providing the mech-
    anism of disaster, represents several of the main relationships of the
    larger play. See Introduction, p. xxvi.

HIERONIMO
    Marry thus: moved with remorse of his misdeeds,
    Ran to a mountain-top and hung himself.   130
BALTHAZAR
    But which of us is to perform that part?
HIERONIMO
    O, that will I my lords, make no doubt of it:
    I'll play the murderer, I warrant you,
    For I already have conceited that.
BALTHAZAR
    And what shall I?   135
HIERONIMO
    Great Soliman the Turkish emperor.
LORENZO
    And I?
HIERONIMO
    Erastus the knight of Rhodes.
BEL-IMPERIA
    And I?
HIERONIMO
    Perseda, chaste and resolute.   140
    And here, my lords, are several abstracts drawn,
    For each of you to note your parts,
    And act it, as occasion's offered you.
    You must provide a Turkish cap,
    A black mustachio and a fauchion.   145
                        Gives a paper to BALTHAZAR
    You with a cross like to a knight of Rhodes.
                        Gives another to LORENZO
    And madam, you must attire yourself
                        He giveth BEL-IMPERIA *another*
    Like Phoebe, Flora, or the Huntress,
    Which to your discretion shall seem best.
    And as for me, my lords, I'll look to one;   150
    And, with the ransom that the viceroy sent
    So furnish and perform this tragedy,
    As all the world shall say Hieronimo
    Was liberal in gracing of it so.

134 *conceited* envisaged, formed a conception of
141 *abstracts* outlines   141 *drawn* drawn up, written out
145 *fauchion* a broad curved sword (also spelled 'falchion')
148 *Huntress* Diana, goddess of hunting
150 *look to* prepare   154 *gracing* setting it out, adorning it

BALTHAZAR
Hieronimo, methinks a comedy were better.   155
HIERONIMO
A comedy?
Fie, comedies are fit for common wits:
But to present a kingly troop withal,
Give me a stately-written tragedy,
Tragedia cothurnata, fitting kings,   160
Containing matter, and not common things.
My lords, all this must be performed,
As fitting for the first night's revelling.
The Italian tragedians were so sharp of wit,
That in one hour's meditation   165
They would perform anything in action.
LORENZO
And well it may; for I have seen the like
In Paris, 'mongst the French tragedians.
HIERONIMO
In Paris? mass, and well remembered!
There's one thing more that rests for us to do.   170
BALTHAZAR
What's that, Hieronimo? forget not anything.
HIERONIMO
Each one of us must act his part
In unknown languages,

156–7 lineation ed. (A . . . wits *one line 1592*)
158 *kingly troop* royal audience
160 *Tragedia cothurnata* in ancient Athens tragedy performed by an
actor wearing buskins (thick-soled boots); the most serious kind
of drama
160 *cothurnata* ed. (*cother nato 1592*)
161 *matter* substance, serious content
170 *rests* remains   173 *unknown* i.e. not in our own tongue

164–6 The reference is to the performers of the *Commedia dell' Arte*,
who improvised plays from scenarios.
172 ff. It is not clear whether the 'sundry languages' will ever have been
used on stage. The note to the reader at IV, iv, 10 s.d. seems to suggest
they were, and that the present text of the playlet is a translation,
perhaps expanded, from the original. Since the audience has already
heard the play's 'argument' they might well have been content to
listen to 'unknown languages', provided they were not given too much
of them and provided the action that accompanied them was highly
explicit and stylised.

That it may breed the more variety.
As you, my lord, in Latin, I in Greek,   175
You in Italian; and for because I know
That Bel-imperia hath practised the French,
In courtly French shall all her phrases be.

BEL-IMPERIA
You mean to try my cunning then, Hieronimo.

BALTHAZAR
But this will be a mere confusion,   180
And hardly shall we all be understood.

HIERONIMO
It must be so, for the conclusion
Shall prove the invention and all was good.
And I myself in an oration,
And with a strange and wondrous show besides,   185
That I will have there behind a curtain,
Assure yourself, shall make the matter known.
And all shall be concluded in one scene,
For there's no pleasure ta'en in tediousness.

BALTHAZAR
[*Aside to* LORENZO] How like you this?   190

LORENZO
Why, thus my lord,
We must resolve to soothe his humours up.

BALTHAZAR
On then Hieronimo, farewell till soon.

HIERONIMO
You'll ply this gear?

LORENZO   I warrant you.
                    Exeunt all but HIERONIMO
HIERONIMO   Why so.
Now shall I see the fall of Babylon,   195
179 *cunning* skill   183 *invention* basic idea
185 *show* tableau (in fact Horatio's body)
185–6 transposed in *1592*   192 *We must resolve* (ends l.191 in *1592*)
192 *soothe . . . up* indulge his whims
194 *ply this gear* carry out this business
194–5 lineation ed. (*one line in 1592*)

---

185 *strange and wondrous show* Horatio's body: the emblem that justifies
   and explains the whole elaborate business.
195 *fall of Babylon* Johnson (pp. 24 ff.) explains that the Geneva Bible
   (in use at Kyd's date of writing) uses 'Babel' both for the Tower of
   Babel and for the wicked city of Babylon: the two would be closely
   associated in the audience's mind. For the destruction of Babylon see
   Isaiah xiii, Jeremiah li, and Revelation xviii.

Wrought by the heavens in this confusion.
And if the world like not this tragedy,
Hard is the hap of old Hieronimo.

Exit

Act IV, Scene ii

Enter ISABELLA *with a weapon*

ISABELLA

Tell me no more! O monstrous homicides!
Since neither piety nor pity moves
The king to justice or compassion,
I will revenge myself upon this place
Where thus they murdered my beloved son.   5
She cuts down the arbour
Down with these branches and these loathsome boughs
Of this unfortunate and fatal pine:
Down with them, Isabella, rent them up
And burn the roots from whence the rest is sprung.
I will not leave a root, a stalk, a tree,   10
A bough, a branch, a blossom, nor a leaf,
No, not an herb within this garden-plot.
Accursed complot of my misery,
Fruitless for ever may this garden be!
Barren the earth, and blissless whosoever   15
Imagines not to keep it unmanured!
An eastern wind commixed with noisome airs
Shall blast the plants and the young saplings;
The earth with serpents shall be pestered,
And passengers, for fear to be infect,   20
Shall stand aloof, and, looking at it, tell,
'There, murdered, died the son of Isabel.'
Ay, here he died, and here I him embrace:

1 s.p. ISABELLA ed. (*not in 1592*)
7 *unfortunate* ominous
8 *rent* rend, tear
13 *complot* plot
16 *unmanured* uncultivated, barren
17 *noisome* pestilent
20 *passengers* passers-by
20 *infect* infected

5 s.d. Isabella may merely strip the leaves and branches from the arbour;
or she may topple a property tree if one was used. See II, iv, 53 s.d.
and note.

See where his ghost solicits with his wounds
Revenge on her that should revenge his death.   25
Hieronimo, make haste to see thy son,
For sorrow and despair hath cited me
To hear Horatio plead with Rhadamanth:
Make haste, Hieronimo, to hold excused
Thy negligence in pursuit of their deaths,   30
Whose hateful wrath bereaved him of his breath.
Ah nay, thou dost delay their deaths,
Forgives the murderers of thy noble son,
And none but I bestir me—to no end.
And as I curse this tree from further fruit,   35
So shall my womb be cursed for his sake;
And with this weapon will I wound the breast,
She stabs herself
The hapless breast that gave Horatio suck.
[Exit]

Act IV, Scene iii

Enter HIERONIMO; *he knocks up the curtain*
Enter the DUKE OF CASTILE

CASTILE
How now Hieronimo, where's your fellows,
That you take all this pain?
HIERONIMO
O sir, it is for the author's credit
To look that all things may go well.
But, good my lord, let me entreat your grace   5

27 *cited* summoned
28 *Rhadamanth* one of the judges of the underworld
29 *hold excused* to *have* it held excused
34 *me—to* ed. (me to *1592*)
1 *fellows* fellow actors

32–4 Even Isabella is deceived by Hieronimo's plan of stealthy and circumspect revenge.
37 s.d., 38 s.d. The stage has to be cleared, though there is no one to remove Isabella's body. Presumably she stumbles off, wounded.
1 s.d. Hieronimo probably hangs a curtain over one of the large entrance-doors at the rear of the Elizabethan stage. We can, it seems clear, take it that there was no permanent inner-stage, at least at this theatre, since such a stage would have been the obvious place to use on this occasion, and stage-carpentry would have been unnecessary.

To give the king the copy of the play:
This is the argument of what we show.

CASTILE
I will, Hieronimo

HIERONIMO
One thing more, my good lord.

CASTILE
What's that?   10

HIERONIMO
Let me entreat your grace
That, when the train are passed into the gallery,
You would vouchsafe to throw me down the key.

CASTILE
I will, Hieronimo.   *Exit* CASTILE

HIERONIMO
What, are you ready, Balthazar?   15
Bring a chair and a cushion for the king.

Enter BALTHAZAR *with a chair*

Well done, Balthazar; hang up the title.
Our scene is Rhodes—what, is your beard on?

BALTHAZAR
Half on, the other is in my hand.

HIERONIMO
Despatch for shame, are you so long?   20

                                    Exit BALTHAZAR

Bethink thyself, Hieronimo,
Recall thy wits, recompt thy former wrongs
Thou hast received by murder of thy son;
And lastly, not least, how Isabel,

7 *argument* plot, narrative
20 *Despatch* hurry   22 *recompt* call to memory

12–13 It would seem natural to use the upper stage for the King and
    courtiers watching the play; subsequent action shows, however, that
    all the actors remained on the main stage. The 'gallery' must refer to
    the 'hall' or 'long gallery' of a large Elizabethan house. 'Throw down' is
    explained by Edwards as 'throw the key down [on the floor] for me.'
17–18 *title . . . scene* There is some evidence that Elizabethan theatres
    used both title-boards and locality-labels to give audiences information
    they might otherwise miss.
18–19 *beard . . . Half on* Kyd deliberately, and with some finesse, makes
    the play-occasion as authentic as possible, and so provides the greatest
    degree of contrast between the surface normality and the horror to
    come: an intensification of the play's continuing irony.

Once his mother and thy dearest wife,   25
All woe-begone for him, hath slain herself.
Behoves thee then, Hieronimo, to be revenged.
The plot is laid of dire revenge:
On then, Hieronimo, pursue revenge,
For nothing wants but acting of revenge.   30

Exit HIERONIMO

Act IV, Seene iv

Enter SPANISH KING, VICEROY, *the* DUKE OF CASTILE, *and their*
train

KING

Now, Viceroy, shall we see the tragedy
Of Soliman the Turkish emperor,
Performed of pleasure by your son the prince,
My nephew Don Lorenzo, and my niece.

VICEROY

Who, Bel-imperia?   5

KING

Ay, and Hieronimo, our marshal,
At whose request they deign to do't themselves:
These be our pastimes in the court of Spain.
Here, brother, you shall be the book-keeper:
This is the argument of that they show.   10

He giveth him a book

Gentlemen, this play of Hieronimo, in sundry languages, was
thought good to be set down in English more largely, for the
easier understanding to every public reader.

Enter BALTHAZAR, BEL-IMPERIA, *and* HIERONIMO

BALTHAZAR

Bashaw, that Rhodes is ours, yield heavens the honour,
And holy Mahomet, our sacred prophet;
And be thou graced with every excellence
That Soliman can give, or thou desire.
But thy desert in conquering Rhodes is less   15

3 *of pleasure* at their pleasure
9 *book-keeper* in the Elizabethan theatre referring to the book-
   holder and prompter
_____

10 s.d. See IV, i, 172 ff. and note.

Than in reserving this fair Christian nymph,
Perseda, blissful lamp of excellence,
Whose eyes compel, like powerful adamant,
The warlike heart of Soliman to wait.

KING

See, Viceroy, that is Balthazar, your son,   20
That represents the emperor Soliman:
How well he acts his amorous passion.

VICEROY

Ay, Bel-imperia hath taught him that.

CASTILE

That's because his mind runs all on Bel-imperia.

HIERONIMO

Whatever joy earth yields betide your majesty.   25

BALTHAZAR

Earth yields no joy without Perseda's love.

HIERONIMO

Let then Perseda on your grace attend.

BALTHAZAR

She shall not wait on me, but I on her:
Drawn by the influence of her lights, I yield.
But let my friend, the Rhodian knight, come forth,   30
Erasto, dearer than my life to me,
That he may see Perseda, my beloved.

Enter [LORENZO *as*] ERASTO

KING

Here comes Lorenzo; look upon the plot,
And tell me, brother, what part plays he?

BEL-IMPERIA

Ah, my Erasto, welcome to Perseda.   35

LORENZO

Thrice happy is Erasto that thou liv'st—
Rhodes' loss is nothing to Erasto's joy;
Sith his Perseda lives, his life survives.

16 *reserving* preserving, protecting
18 *adamant* the loadstone (which had magnetic properties)
19 *wait* attend on her
29 *lights* eyes
33 *plot* synopsis and cast-list
37 *to* compared to

20–4 Kyd takes some pains to see that the audience is aware of the parallels
between the actor and his assumed part.

BALTHAZAR
Ah, bashaw, here is love between Erasto
And fair Perseda, sovereign of my soul.   40
HIERONIMO
Remove Erasto, mighty Soliman,
And then Perseda will be quickly won.
BALTHAZAR
Erasto is my friend, and while he lives
Perseda never will remove her love.
HIERONIMO
Let not Erasto live to grieve great Soliman.   45
BALTHAZAR
Dear is Erasto in our princely eye.
HIERONIMO
But if he be your rival, let him die.
BALTHAZAR
Why, let him die: so love commandeth me.
Yet grieve I that Erasto should so die.
HIERONIMO
Erasto, Soliman saluteth thee,   50
And lets thee wit by me his highness' will,
Which is, thou shouldst be thus employed.
                                                    Stab him
BEL-IMPERIA   *Ay me,*
Erasto! see, Soliman, Erasto's slain!
BALTHAZAR
Yet liveth Soliman to comfort thee.
Fair queen of beauty, let not favour die,   55
But with a gracious eye behold his grief,
That with Perseda's beauty is increased,
If by Perseda his grief be not released.
BEL-IMPERIA
Tyrant, desist soliciting vain suits;
Relentless are mine ears to thy laments,   60
As thy butcher is pitiless and base,
Which seized on my Erasto, harmless knight.
Yet by thy power thou thinkest to command,
And to thy power Perseda doth obey:
But were she able, thus she would revenge   65

52 *Ay me*, ed. (*begins l.53 in 1592*)
55 *favour* i.e. your love
58 *Perseda his* ed. (Persedaes *1592*) 'his' must be heavily elided, as
   the *1592* spelling indicates

Thy treacheries on thee, ignoble prince: *Stab him*
And on herself she would be thus revenged   *Stab herself*
KING
Well said, old marshal, this was bravely done!
HIERONIMO
But Bel-imperia plays Perseda well.
VICEROY
Were this in earnest, Bel-imperia,   70
You would be better to my son than so.
KING
But now what follows for Hieronimo?
HIERONIMO
Marry, this follows for Hieronimo:
Here break we off our sundry languages
And thus conclude I in our vulgar tongue.   75
Haply you think, but bootless are your thoughts,
That this is fabulously counterfeit,
And that we do as all tragedians do:
To die today, for fashioning our scene,
The death of Ajax, or some Roman peer,   80
And in a minute starting up again,
Revive to please to-morrow's audience.
No, princes; know I am Hieronimo,
The hopeless father of a hapless son,
Whose tongue is tuned to tell his latest tale,   85
Not to excuse gross errors in the play.
I see your looks urge instance of these words;
Behold the reason urging me to this:
                                              Shows his dead son
See here my show, look on this spectacle.

75 *vulgar tongue* the vernacular, our everyday speech
76 *Haply* perhaps
76 *bootless* unavailing
77 *fabulously counterfeit* acted in fiction only
79 *for . . . scene* ed. (for (fashioning our scene) *1592*) enacting our play
85 *latest* last
87 *instance* explanation, what lies behind (these words)
89 *show* tableau, spectacle

68 *Well said* The King refers to Hieronimo's success in composing the piece: 'Well done'.
76–86 The fiction—fact relationship, stated very simply here by Kyd, became a topic for much more subtle exploration by Shakespeare and later Elizabethan dramatists.

Here lay my hope, and here my hope hath end;   90
Here lay my heart, and here my heart was slain;
Here lay my treasure, here my treasure lost;
Here lay my bliss, and here my bliss bereft;
But hope, heart, treasure, joy, and bliss,
All fled, failed, died, yea, all decayed with this.   95
From forth these wounds came breath that gave me life;
They murdered me that made these fatal marks.
The cause was love, whence grew this mortal hate
The hate, Lorenzo and young Balthazar,
The love, my son to Bel-imperia.   100
But night, the coverer of accursed crimes,
With pitchy silence hushed these traitors' harms
And lent them leave, for they had sorted leisure
To take advantage in my garden-plot
Upon my son, my dear Horatio: 105
There merciless they butchered up my boy,
In black dark night, to pale dim cruel death.
He shrieks, I heard, and yet methinks I hear,
His dismal outcry echo in the air.
With soonest speed I hasted to the noise,   110
Where hanging on a tree I found my son,
Through-girt with wounds, and slaughtered as you see.
And grieved I, think you, at this spectacle?
Speak, Portuguese, whose loss resembles mine:
If thou canst weep upon thy Balthazar,   115
'Tis like I wailed for my Horatio.
And you, my lord, whose reconciled son
Marched in a net, and thought himself unseen,
And rated me for brainsick lunacy,
With 'God amend that mad Hieronimo!'—   120
How can you brook our play's catastrophe?
And here behold this bloody handkercher,
Which at Horatio's death I weeping dipped

102 *harms* their malicious actions   103 *sorted* sought out
112 *Through-girt* pierced through
118 *Marched in a net* kept himself concealed, practised deceit; a pro-
    verbial phrase
119 *rated* berated

96 *From forth . . . life* i.e. *my* life-breath left me when these wounds were
   made in my son's body.
117 *reconciled* presumably to Hieronimo (see III, xiv, 130–64).
119–20 Compare Lorenzo's advice to the King at III, xii, 85–9 and 96–8.

Within the river of his bleeding wounds:
It as propitious, see I have reserved,   125
And never hath it left my bloody heart,
Soliciting remembrance of my vow
With these, O these accursed murderers:
Which now performed, my heart is satisfied.
And to this end the bashaw I became   130
That might revenge me on Lorenzo's life,
Who therefore was appointed to the part,
And was to represent the knight of Rhodes,
That I might kill him more conveniently.
So, Viceroy, was this Balthazar, thy son—   135
That Soliman which Bel-imperia
In person of Perseda murdered—
Solely appointed to that tragic part
That she might slay him that offended her.
Poor Bel-imperia missed her part in this: 140
For though the story saith she should have died,
Yet I of kindness, and of care to her,
Did otherwise determine of her end;
But love of him whom they did hate too much
Did urge her resolution to be such.   145
And princes, now behold Hieronimo,
Author and actor in this tragedy,
Bearing his latest fortune in his fist:
And will as resolute conclude his part
As any of the actors gone before.   150
And, gentles, thus I end my play:
Urge no more words; I have no more to say.

He runs to hang himself

KING
O hearken, Viceroy! Hold, Hieronimo!
Brother, my nephew and thy son are slain!

---

125 *propitious* of good omen; a token prompting to due revenge
140 *missed her part* strayed from her assigned part
153 *Hold, Hieronimo!* ed. (holde *Hieronimo, 1592*) wait, Hieronimo;
      'hold' in *1592* might mean 'arrest'

130–52 This may be over-explicit; but audiences are notoriously slow at
   registering the action of plays, especially when they have more than one
   group of actors to watch, as is the case with Hieronimo's playlet and
   its audience.

VICEROY

We are betrayed! my Balthazar is slain!   155
Break ope the doors, run, save Hieronimo.
    [*They break in, and hold* HIERONIMO]
Hieronimo, do but inform the king of these events;
Upon mine honour thou shalt have no harm.

HIERONIMO

Viceroy, I will not trust thee with my life,
Which I this day have offered to my son.   160
Accursed wretch,
Why stayest thou him that was resolved to die?

KING

Speak, traitor; damned, bloody murderer, speak!
For now I have thee I will make thee speak—
Why hast thou done this undeserving deed?   165

VICEROY

Why hast thou murdered my Balthazar?

CASTILE

Why hast thou butchered both my children thus?

HIERONIMO

O, good words!
As dear to me was my Horatio
As yours, or yours, or yours, my lord, to you.   170
My guiltless son was by Lorenzo slain,
And by Lorenzo and that Balthazar

161 *Accursed wretch*, ed. (*begins l.162 in 1592*)
168 *O, good words* ed. (*begins l.169 in 1592*)
172 *by* i.e. by the deaths of

---

156 The doors have been locked by Castile, as Hieronimo requested
 (IV, iii, 12–13). The attendants 'break in' from off-stage and guard
 Hieronimo.
165–7 and 179–82 Edwards finds the questions at these points an 'extraordinary inconsistency', since Hieronimo has already 'told [the king]
 everything'. He accounts for the inconsistency by supposing (with
 Schücking) that IV, iv, 153–201 represents 'an alternative ending
 to the play', replacing Hieronimo's long speech (ll.73–152), and
 requiring therefore the brief explanation at ll.169 ff. Edwards makes
 out a good case, but the inconsistency may be less glaring than at first
 appears, for at l.179 the King is asking Hieronimo to discuss his confederates (Bel-imperia principally), which he has not yet done in
 detail; Hieronimo refuses to break the vow he swore to Bel-imperia at
 IV, i, 42–5 (see ll.187–8). The King's earlier questioning, and that of
 the Viceroy and Castile, might be explained as the result of grief-
 stricken bewilderment and not mere redundancy; they have not taken
 in what Hieronimo has said.

Am I at last revenged thoroughly,
Upon whose souls may heavens be yet avenged
With greater far than these afflictions.   175

CASTILE
But who were thy confederates in this?

VICEROY
That was thy daughter Bel-imperia;
For by her hand my Balthazar was slain:
I saw her stab him.

KING   Why speak'st thou not?

HIERONIMO
What lesser liberty can kings afford   180
Than harmless silence? then afford it me:
Sufficeth I may not, nor I will not tell thee.

KING
Fetch forth the tortures.
Traitor as thou art, I'll make thee tell.

HIERONIMO   Indeed,
Thou may'st torment me, as his wretched son   185
Hath done in murdering my Horatio,
But never shalt thou force me to reveal
The thing which I have vowed inviolate.
And therefore in despite of all thy threats,
Pleased with their deaths, and eased with their revenge,   190
First take my tongue, and afterwards my heart.
                              [*He bites out his tongue*]

KING
O monstrous resolution of a wretch!
See, Viceroy, he hath bitten forth his tongue
Rather than to reveal what we required.

CASTILE
Yet can he write.   195

KING
And if in this he satisfy us not,

---

184 *Indeed* ed. (*begins l.185 in 1592*)

191 s.d. Barish (p. 82) thinks this action 'betrays the final despair at the
    uselessness of talk, the beserk resolve to have done with language
    forever.' Johnson (p. 34) says it 'serves to identify Hieronimo as ad-
    mirably stoic' since his action imitates Zeno of Elea, the famous Stoic,
    who under torture 'bit off his own tongue, and spat it out in the tor-
    mentors' face' (quoting William Baldwin's *Treatise of Morall Philosophie*,
    9th ed., 1579).

We will devise th'extremest kind of death
That ever was invented for a wretch.
                Then he makes signs for a knife to mend his pen

CASTILE

O, he would have a knife to mend his pen.

VICEROY

Here; and advise thee that thou write the troth.   200

KING

Look to my brother! save Hieronimo!
                He with a knife stabs the DUKE *and himself*
What age hath ever heard such monstrous deeds?
My brother, and the whole succeeding hope
That Spain expected after my decease!
Go bear his body hence, that we may mourn   205
The loss of our beloved brother's death;
That he may be entombed, whate'er befall:
I am the next, the nearest, last of all.

VICEROY

And thou, Don Pedro, do the like for us;
Take up our hapless son, untimely slain: 210
Set me with him, and he with woeful me,
Upon the main-mast of a ship unmanned,
And let the wind and tide haul me along
To Scylla's barking and untamed gulf,
Or to the loathsome pool of Acheron,   215
To weep my want for my sweet Balthazar:
Spain hath no refuge for a Portingale.

The trumpets sound a dead march, the KING *of* SPAIN *mourning
after his brother's body, and the* VICEROY *of* PORTINGALE *bearing
                the body of his son*

200 *advise thee* be advised, take care
201 s.p. KING ed. (*not in 1592*)
213 *haul* drive; hale; possibly, suggests Edwards, a word with nautical
      associations for Kyd
214 *gulf* ed. (greefe *1592*)
215 *Acheron* see I, i, 19 and note   216 *my want for* my loss of
217 s.d. VICEROY OF PORTINGALE ed. (*King of Portingale 1592*)

202–4 Patriotic feelings may be involved here: English audiences would be
      delighted by Spain's discomfiture.
214 *Scylla's . . . gulf* Scylla was one of a pair of dangerous rocks (the other
      was Charybdis) between Italy and Sicily; Joseph says that Homer
      refers to Scylla, the goddess of the rock, as 'barking', while later
      writers described her as accompanied by barking dogs.

Act IV, Scene v

Ghost [of ANDREA] *and* REVENGE

ANDREA

Ay, now my hopes have end in their effects,
When blood and sorrow finish my desires:
Horatio murdered in his father's bower,
Vild Serberine by Pedringano slain,
False Pedringano hanged by quaint device,   5
Fair Isabella by herself misdone,
Prince Balthazar by Bel-imperia stabbed,
The Duke of Castile and his wicked son
Both done to death by old Hieronimo,
My Bel-imperia fallen as Dido fell,   10
And good Hieronimo slain by himself:
Ay, these were spectacles to please my soul.
Now will I beg at lovely Proserpine,
That, by the virtue of her princely doom,
I may consort my friends in pleasing sort,   15
And on my foes work just and sharp revenge.
I'll lead my friend Horatio through those fields
Where never-dying wars are still inured:
I'll lead fair Isabella to that train
Where pity weeps but never feeleth pain: 20
I'll lead my Bel-imperia to those joys
That vestal virgins and fair queens possess;
I'll lead Hieronimo where Orpheus plays,

1 s.p. ANDREA ed. (*Ghoast. 1592 throughout this scene*)
1 s.d. *Ghost* ed. (*Enter Ghoast 1592*)
4 *Vild* vile   5 *quaint* cunning
6 *misdone* slain
14 *doom* judgment
15 *consort* accompany, treat
18 *inured* carried on
19 *train* company
22 *vestal virgins* virgins consecrated to the Roman goddess Vesta,
   and vowed to chastity
23 *Orpheus* see III, xiii, 117 and note

1–2 Compare Revenge at II, vi, 7–8.
10 *as Dido fell* Vergil (*Aeneid* IV) records that Dido killed herself after
   Aeneas's departure from Carthage. The legend Vergil adapted also
   speaks of Dido as a suicide, killing herself to avoid marriage with
   Iarbas.

Adding sweet pleasure to eternal days.
But say, Revenge, for thou must help, or none,   25
Against the rest how shall my hate be shown?

REVENGE

This hand shall hale them down to deepest hell,
Where none but Furies, bugs and tortures dwell.

ANDREA

Then, sweet Revenge, do this at my request;
Let me be judge, and doom them to unrest: 30
Let loose poor Tityus from the vulture's gripe,
And let Don Cyprian supply his room;
Place Don Lorenzo on Ixion's wheel,
And let the lover's endless pains surcease—
Juno forgets old wrath, and grants him ease;   35
Hang Balthazar about Chimaera's neck,
And let him there bewail his bloody love,
Repining at our joys that are above;
Let Serberine go roll the fatal stone,
And take from Sisyphus his endless moan;   40
False Pedringano for his treachery,
Let him be dragged through boiling Acheron,
And there live, dying still in endless flames,
Blaspheming gods and all their holy names.

REVENGE

Then haste we down to meet thy friends and foes: 45
To place thy friends in ease, the rest in woes.
For here, though death hath end their misery,
I'll there begin their endless tragedy.   *Exeunt*

---

28 *bugs* bugbears, horrors
32 *supply his room* take his place
34 *the lover* Ixion, who had tried to seduce Juno
34 *surcease* cease
36 *Chimaera* a fire-breathing monster of Greek mythology, with head of a lion, body of a goat, tail of a dragon
40 *Sisyphus* a legendary king of Crete, condemned for his misdeeds to roll a large stone eternally uphill in the underworld
43 *still* continually, for ever
47 *end* ended

---

32 *Don Cyprian* the Duke of Castile; he had frowned on Andrea's relationship with Bel-imperia (see II, i, 45–8).

Scenes added to
THE SPANISH TRAGEDY
in the edition of 1602

First Addition, between II, v, 45 and 46. (p. 45)

[For outrage fits our cursed wretchedness.]
Ay me, Hieronimo, sweet husband speak.
HIERONIMO
He supped with us tonight, frolic and merry,
And said he would go visit Balthazar
At the duke's palace: there the prince doth lodge.
He had no custom to stay out so late,   5
He may be in his chamber; some go see.
Roderigo, ho!

Enter PEDRO *and* JAQUES

ISABELLA
Ay me, he raves. Sweet Hieronimo!
HIERONIMO
True, all Spain takes note of it.
Besides, he is so generally beloved   10
His majesty the other day did grace him
With waiting on his cup: these be favours
Which do assure he cannot be short-lived.
ISABELLA
Sweet Hieronimo!
HIERONIMO
I wonder how this fellow got his clothes?   15
Sirrah, sirrah, I'll know the truth of all:
Jaques, run to the Duke of Castile's presently,
And bid my son Horatio to come home:
I and his mother have had strange dreams tonight.
Do you hear me, sir?
JAQUES   Ay, sir.

2 *frolic* frolicsome, gay
7 *Roderigo, ho!* (*ends l.6 in 1602*)
10 *generally* by everyone
13 *assure* ensure, prove
13 *he* ed. (me *1602*)
17 *presently* at once

11–12 See I, iv, 130.
6

HIERONIMO   Well sir, begone.   20
  Pedro, come hither: knowest thou who this is?
PEDRO
  Too well, sir.
HIERONIMO
  Too well? Who? Who is it? Peace, Isabella:
  Nay, blush not, man.
PEDRO   It is my lord Horatio.
HIERONIMO
  Ha, ha! Saint James, but this doth make me laugh,   25
  That there are more deluded than myself.
PEDRO
  Deluded?
HIERONIMO
  Ay, I would have sworn myself within this hour
  That this had been my son Horatio,
  His garments are so like.   30
  Ha! are they not great persuasions?
ISABELLA
  O, would to God it were not so!
HIERONIMO
  Were not, Isabella? Dost thou dream it is?
  Can thy soft bosom entertain a thought
  That such a black deed of mischief should be done   35
  On one so pure and spotless as our son?
  Away, I am ashamed.
ISABELLA   Dear Hieronimo,
  Cast a more serious eye upon thy grief:
  Weak apprehension gives but weak belief.
HIERONIMO
  It was a man, sure, that was hanged up here;   40
  A youth, as I remember: I cut him down.
  If it should prove my son now after all—
  Say you, say you, light! Lend me a taper,
  Let me look again. O God!
  Confusion, mischief, torment, death and hell,   45

20–4 lineation ed. (*prose in 1602*)
30–1 lineation ed. (*one line 1602*)
31 *persuasions* evidences, means of persuasion
36 *pure* ed. (poore *1602*)
37 *Dear Hieronimo* ed. (*begins l.38 in 1602*)
39 *apprehension* understanding, grasp of what's happening
44 *O God!* ed. (*begins l.45 in 1602*)

Drop all your stings at once in my cold bosom,
That now is stiff with horror; kill me quickly:
Be gracious to me, thou infective night,
And drop this deed of murder down on me;
Gird in my waste of grief with thy large darkness,   50
And let me not survive to see the light
May put me in the mind I had a son.

ISABELLA

O, sweet Horatio. O, my dearest son!

HIERONIMO

How strangely had I lost my way to grief!
[Sweet lovely rose, ill plucked before thy time,]

Second Addition, replacing III, ii, 65 and part of 66. (p. 55)

[LORENZO

Why so, Hieronimo? use me.]

HIERONIMO

Who, you, my lord?
I reserve your favour for a greater honour;
This is a very toy my lord, a toy.

LORENZO

All's one, Hieronimo, acquaint me with it.

HIERONIMO

I'faith, my lord, 'tis an idle thing.   5
I must confess, I ha' been too slack,
Too tardy. Too remiss unto your honour.

LORENZO

How now, Hieronimo?

HIERONIMO

In troth, my lord, it is a thing of nothing,
The murder of a son, or so: 10
A thing of nothing, my lord.

[LORENZO   Why then, farewell.]

48 *infective* bearing infection
50 *Gird in* confine, limit
50 *waste* a vast, empty area (with a play on 'waist')
 3 *toy* trifle, trivial thing
5–7 lineation ed. (*prose in 1602*)

Third Addition, between III, xi, 1 and 2. (p. 79)

[1 PORTINGALE
   By your leave, sir.]
HIERONIMO
    'Tis neither as you think, nor as you think,
    Nor as you think: you're wide all:
    These slippers are not mine, they were my son Horatio's.
    My son, and what's a son? A thing begot
    Within a pair of minutes, thereabout: 5
    A lump bred up in darkness, and doth serve
    To ballace these light creatures we call women;
    And, at nine moneths' end, creeps forth to light.
    What is there yet in a son
    To make a father dote, rave or run mad?   10
    Being born, it pouts, cries, and breeds teeth.
    What is there yet in a son? He must be fed,
    Be taught to go, and speak. Ay, or yet?
    Why might not a man love a calf as well?
    Or melt in passion o'er a frisking kid,   15
    As for a son? Methinks a young bacon
    Or a fine little smooth horse-colt
    Should move a man as much as doth a son:
    For one of these in very little time
    Will grow to some good use, whereas a son,   20
    The more he grows in stature and in years,
    The more unsquared, unbevelled he appears,
    Reckons his parents among the rank of fools,
    Strikes care upon their heads with his mad riots,
    Makes them look old before they meet with age: 25

---

2 *wide* wide of the mark, quite wrong
4 *A thing begot* ed. (*begins l.5 in 1602*)
7 *ballace* ballast, weigh down
8 *moneths* months (metre requires a dissyllable)
11 *breeds teeth* cuts teeth
13 *go* walk
16 *young bacon* piglet

---

13 *Ay, or yet?* Hieronimo means 'Yes, or what else?', 'What can I add?'
22 *unsquared, unbevelled* Boas says 'uneven and unpolished': the author
   of this Addition has in mind the rough manners of young bloods.
   'Bevelling' is a decorative process in carpentry performed with a 'bevel'
   or 'bevel-square'.

This is a son:
And what a loss were this, considered truly?
Oh, but my Horatio
Grew out of reach of these insatiate humours:
He loved his loving parents, 30
He was my comfort, and his mother's joy,
The very arm that did hold up our house:
Our hopes were stored up in him,
None but a damned murderer could hate him.
He had not seen the back of nineteen year, 35
When his strong arm unhorsed the proud Prince Balthazar,
And his great mind, too full of honour,
Took him unto mercy,
That valiant but ignoble Portingale.
Well, heaven is heaven still, 40
And there is Nemesis and Furies,
And things called whips,
And they sometimes do meet with murderers:
They do not always 'scape, that's some comfort.
Ay, ay, ay, and then time steals on: 45
And steals, and steals, till violence leaps forth
Like thunder wrapped in a ball of fire,
And so doth bring confusion to them all.
[Good leave have you: nay, I pray you go,]

26–30 lineation ed. (This . . . truly. / O . . . of these / Insatiate . . .
   parents, *1602*)
29 *insatiate humours* unsatisfied whims and caprices
35 *the back of* i.e. he was still nineteen
38 *unto* ed. (vs to *1602*)
38–9 lineation ed. (*one line 1602*)
41 *Nemesis* a personification of the gods' anger at human presumption, and their punishment of it
41 *Furies* legendary avengers of crime in ancient Greece
45–7 lineation ed. (I, . . . steales, and steales / Till . . . thunder /
   Wrapt . . . fire, *1602*)
48 *confusion* destruction

36–9 The syntax is unclear at this point. Presumably l.39 simply expands
'the proud Prince Balthazar' (l.36). Should l.39 follow l.36 immediately?

Fourth Addition, between III, xii and xiii (p. 85)

Enter JAQUES *and* PEDRO

JAQUES
    I wonder, Pedro, why our master thus
    At midnight sends us with our torches' light,
    When man and bird and beast are all at rest,
    Save those that watch for rape and bloody murder?
PEDRO
    O Jaques, know thou that our master's mind   5
    Is much distraught since his Horatio died,
    And now his aged years should sleep in rest,
    His heart in quiet; like a desperate man,
    Grows lunatic and childish for his son:
    Sometimes, as he doth at his table sit,   10
    He speaks as if Horatio stood by him;
    Then starting in a rage, falls on the earth,
    Cries out 'Horatio, where is my Horatio?'
    So that with extreme grief and cutting sorrow,
    There is not left in him one inch of man: 15
    See, where he comes.

Enter HIERONIMO

HIERONIMO
    I pry through every crevice of each wall,
    Look on each tree, and search through every brake,
    Beat at the bushes, stamp our grandam earth,
    Dive in the water, and stare up to heaven,   20
    Yet cannot I behold my son Horatio.
    How now, who's there, sprites, sprites?
PEDRO
    We are your servants that attend you, sir.
HIERONIMO
    What make you with your torches in the dark?
PEDRO
    You bid us light them, and attend you here.   25
HIERONIMO
    No, no, you are deceived, not I, you are deceived:

12 *starting* starting up
17 *crevice* (creuie *1602*)
18 *brake* thicket
22 *sprites, sprites?* ed. (sprits, sprits? *1602*) spirits, demons
24 *What make you* What are you doing? What is your purpose?

Was I so mad to bid you light your torches now?
Light me your torches at the mid of noon,
Whenas the sun-god rides in all his glory:
Light me your torches then.

PEDRO   Then we burn daylight.   30

HIERONIMO
Let it be burnt: night is a murderous slut,
That would not have her treasons to be seen;
And yonder pale-faced Hecate there, the moon,
Doth give consent to that is done in darkness;
And all those stars that gaze upon her face,   35
Are aglets on her sleeve, pins on her train;
And those that should be powerful and divine,
Do sleep in darkness when they most should shine.

PEDRO
Provoke them not, fair sir, with tempting words:
The heavens are gracious, and your miseries   40
And sorrow makes you speak you know not what.

HIERONIMO
Villain, thou liest, and thou doest naught
But tell me I am mad: thou liest, I am not mad.
I know thee to be Pedro, and he Jaques.
I'll prove it to thee, and were I mad, how could I?   45
Where was she that same night when my Horatio
Was murdered? She should have shone: search thou the
    book.
Had the moon shone, in my boy's face there was a kind of
    grace,
That I know (nay, I do know) had the murderer seen him,

29 *Whenas* when
30 *burn daylight* a phrase meaning to waste time; here used also in
    the literal sense
33 *Hecate* ed. (Hee-cat *1602*) in Greek thought · goddess associ-
    ated with night and the lower world; Elizabethans associated
    her with the moon. Here, two syllables only
36 *aglets* ed. (aggots *1602*) spangles ('properly, the ornamental tags
    of laces', Edwards)
36 *pins* spangles, ornaments
41 *And sorrow* ed. (*ends l.40 in 1602*)
47 *Was murdered* ed. (*ends l.46 in 1602*)
47 *book* almanac, recording the phases of the moon
49 *That I know* ed. (*ends l.48 in 1602*)

45 *prove it* i.e. prove the Heavens negligent in the matter of Horatio's
    murder.

His weapon would have fallen and cut the earth,   50
Had he been framed of naught but blood and death.
Alack, when mischief doth it knows not what,
What shall we say to mischief?

Enter ISABELLA

ISABELLA
Dear Hieronimo, come in a-doors.
O, seek not means so to increase thy sorrow.   55
HIERONIMO
Indeed, Isabella, we do nothing here;
I do not cry; ask Pedro, and ask Jaques;
Not I indeed, we are very merry, very merry.
ISABELLA
How? be merry here, be merry here?
Is not this the place, and this the very tree,   60
Where my Horatio died, where he was murdered?
HIERONIMO
Was—do not say what: let her weep it out.
This was the tree, I set it of a kernel,
And when our hot Spain could not let it grow,
But that the infant and the human sap   65
Began to wither, duly twice a morning
Would I be sprinkling it with fountain water.
At last it grew, and grew, and bore and bore,
Till at the length
It grew a gallows, and did bear our son.   70
It bore thy fruit and mine: O wicked, wicked plant.
                      One knocks within at the door
See who knock there.
PEDRO   It is a painter, sir.
HIERONIMO
Bid him come in, and paint some comfort,
For surely there's none lives but painted comfort.
Let him come in. One knows not what may chance: 75

51 *framed* made, created
61 *died* ed. (hied *1602*)
69 *Till . . . length* ed. (*begins l.70 in 1602*)
74 *painted* false, merely apparent

64 ff. *our hot Spain* a much stronger sense of actual locality than in Kyd's
text.

God's will that I should set this tree—but even so
Masters ungrateful servants rear from naught,
And then they hate them that did bring them up.

Enter the PAINTER

PAINTER
God bless you, sir.
HIERONIMO
Wherefore? why, thou scornful villain,   80
How, where, or by what means should I be blessed?
ISABELLA
What wouldst thou have, good fellow?
PAINTER   Justice, madam.
HIERONIMO
O ambitious beggar, wouldst thou have that
That lives not in the world?
Why, all the undelved mines cannot buy   85
An ounce of justice, 'tis a jewel so inestimable:
I tell thee,
God hath engrossed all justice in his hands,
And there is none, but what comes from him.
PAINTER
O then I see   90
That God must right me for my murdered son.
HIERONIMO
How, was thy son murdered?
PAINTER
Ay sir, no man did hold a son so dear.
HIERONIMO
What, not as thine? that's a lie
As massy as the earth: I had a son,   95

76 *but even so* ed. (*begins l.77 in 1602*)
80 *Wherefore? Why?*
85 *undelved* unworked
87 *I tell thee* ed. (*begins l.88 in 1602*)
88 *engrossed* taken up
90 *O then I see* ed. (*begins l.91 in 1602*)
95 *massy* huge, weighty

───────────────────────────────────────

76–7 The dash in l.76 represents the anguished question implied in the
   preceding phrase: 'Can it also be God's will that it should grow to
   such terrible uses?'
90–4 The writer of this Addition develops Kyd's device of including a
   surrogate for Hieronimo, 'The lively portrait of my dying self' (III,
   xiii, 85).

Whose least unvalued hair did weigh
A thousand of thy sons: and he was murdered.

PAINTER

Alas sir, I had no more but he.

HIERONIMO

Nor I, nor I: but this same one of mine
Was worth a legion: but all is one.   100
Pedro, Jaques, go in a-doors: Isabella go,
And this good fellow here and I
Will range this hideous orchard up and down,
Like to two lions reaved of their young.
Go in a-doors, I say.   105

Exeunt [ISABELLA, PEDRO, JAQUES]
The PAINTER *and he sits down*

Come, let's talk wisely now. Was thy son murdered?

PAINTER

Ay sir.

HIERONIMO

So was mine. How dost take it? Art thou not sometimes
mad? Is there no tricks that comes before thine eyes?

PAINTER

O Lord, yes sir.   110

HIERONIMO

Art a painter? Canst paint me a tear, or a wound, a groan, or
a sigh? Canst paint me such a tree as this?

PAINTER

Sir, I am sure you have heard of my painting, my name's
Bazardo.

HIERONIMO

Bazardo! afore God, an excellent fellow! Look you sir, do   115
you see, I'd have you paint me in my gallery, in your oil
colours matted, and draw me five years younger than I am.
Do you see sir, let five years go, let them go, like the marshal
of Spain. My wife Isabella standing by me, with a speaking
look to my son Horatio, which should intend to this or some   120

---

100 *all is one* no matter
103 *range* walk up and down
104 *reaved* bereft, robbed
116 *me in my* ed. (me my *1602*)
117 *matted* perhaps 'made dull or matt'; but Boas may be right in
      suggesting 'set in a mat or mount'
119 *speaking* eloquent, full of meaning
120 *intend to* signify

such like purpose: 'God bless thee, my sweet son': and my
hand leaning upon his head, thus, sir, do you see? may it
be done?

PAINTER

Very well sir.

HIERONIMO

Nay, I pray mark me sir. Then sir, would I have you paint   125
me this tree, this very tree. Canst paint a doleful cry?

PAINTER

Seemingly, sir.

HIERONIMO

Nay, it should cry: but all is one. Well sir, paint me a youth
run through and through with villains' swords, hanging
upon this tree. Canst thou draw a murderer?   130

PAINTER

I'll warrant you sir, I have the pattern of the most notorious
villains that ever lived in all Spain.

HIERONIMO

O, let them be worse, worse: stretch thine art, and let their
beards be of Judas his own colour, and let their eyebrows
jutty over: in any case observe that. Then sir, after some   135
violent noise, bring me forth in my shirt, and my gown under
mine arm, with my torch in my hand, and my sword reared
up thus: and with these words:
    What noise is this? who calls Hieronimo?
May it be done?   140

PAINTER

Yea sir.

HIERONIMO

Well sir, then bring me forth, bring me through alley and
alley, still with a distracted countenance going along, and
let my hair heave up my night-cap. Let the clouds scowl,
make the moon dark, the stars extinct, the winds blowing,   145
the bells tolling, the owl shrieking, the toads croaking, the
minutes jarring, and the clock striking twelve. And then at

127 *Seemingly* in illusion
131 *pattern* model, portrait
134 *Judas . . . colour* red (Judas Iscariot was alleged to be red-haired)
135 *jutty* project
142 s.p. ʜɪᴇʀᴏɴɪᴍᴏ ed. (*not in 1602*)
147 *jarring* ed. (iering *1602*) ticking away

135–9 These lines may provide us with a good indication of Elizabethan
    practice in staging the first lines of II, v in the main play.

last, sir, starting, behold a man hanging: and tottering, and
tottering as you know the wind will weave a man, and I
with a trice to cut him down. And looking upon him by the   150
advantage of my torch, find it to be my son Horatio. There
you may show a passion, there you may show a passion.
Draw me like old Priam of Troy, crying 'The house is a-fire,
the house is a-fire as the torch over my head!' Make me
curse, make me rave, make me cry, make me mad, make me   155
well again, make me curse hell, invocate heaven, and in the
end leave me in a trance; and so forth.

PAINTER
And is this the end?

HIERONIMO
O no, there is no end: the end is death and madness! As I
am never better than when I am mad, then methinks I am a   160
brave fellow, then I do wonders: but reason abuseth me, and
there's the torment, there's the hell. At the last, sir, bring me
to one of the murderers, were he as strong as Hector, thus
would I tear and drag him up and down.

He beats the PAINTER *in, then comes out again with a book in his
hand*

Fifth Addition, replacing IV, iv, 168 to 190. (pp. 120–1)

[CASTILE
Why hast thou butchered both my children thus?]

HIERONIMO
But are you sure they are dead?

CASTILE   Ay, slave, too sure.

HIERONIMO
What, and yours too?

VICEROY
Ay, all are dead, not one of them survive.

148 *tottering* dangling, swinging to and fro
149 *weave* weave about, make him swing (*O.E.D.* does not give this
        transitive sense)
150 *with a trice* instantly
151 *advantage* assistance
152 *show* ed. (*not in 1602*)
161 *brave* glorious, splendid
161 *abuseth* deceives

153–7 The closeness of these lines to the First Player's speech (*Hamlet*
II, ii) is intriguing.

HIERONIMO
    Nay then, I care not, come, and we shall be friends:
    Let us lay our heads together;   5
    See here's a goodly noose will hold them all.
VICEROY
    O damned devil, how secure he is.
HIERONIMO
    Secure, why dost thou wonder at it?
    I tell thee Viceroy, this day I have seen revenge,
    And in that sight am grown a prouder monarch   10
    Than ever sat under the crown of Spain:
    Had I as many lives as there be stars,
    As many heavens to go to as those lives,
    I'd give them all, ay, and my soul to boot,
    But I would see thee ride in this red pool.   15
CASTILE
    Speak, who were thy confederates in this?
VICEROY
    That was thy daughter Bel-imperia,
    For by her hand my Balthazar was slain:
    I saw her stab him.
HIERONIMO   Oh, good words:
    As dear to me was my Horatio,   20
    As yours, or yours, or yours, my lord, to you.
    My guiltless son was by Lorenzo slain,
    And by Lorenzo, and that Balthazar,
    Am I at last revenged thoroughly,
    Upon whose souls may heavens be yet revenged   25
    With greater far than these afflictions.
    Methinks since I grew inward with revenge,
    I cannot look with scorn enough on death.
KING
    What, dost thou mock us, slave? Bring tortures forth.

  7 *secure* confident
  9 *revenge* ed. (reueng'd *1602*)
14 *to boot* in addition
19 *Oh, good words:* ed. (*begins l.20 in 1602*)
27 *inward with* closely acquainted with
29 *tortures* instruments of torture

HIERONIMO

    Do, do, do, and meantime I'll torture you.   30
    You had a son, as I take it: and your son
    Should ha' been married to your daughter:
    Ha, was't not so? You had a son too,
    He was my liege's nephew. He was proud,
    And politic. Had he lived, he might ha' come   35
    To wear the crown of Spain, I think 'twas so:
    'Twas I that killed him; look you, this same hand,
    'Twas it that stabbed his heart; do you see, this hand?
    For one Horatio, if you ever knew him, a youth,
    One that they hanged up in his father's garden,   40
    One that did force your valiant son to yield,
    While your more valiant son did take him prisoner.

VICEROY

    Be deaf my senses, I can hear no more.

KING

    Fall heaven, and cover us with thy sad ruins.

CASTILE

    Roll all the world within thy pitchy cloud.   45

HIERONIMO

    Now do I applaud what I have acted.
              Nunc iners cadat manus.
    Now to express the rupture of my part,
    [First take my tongue, and afterward my heart.]

END

35 *ha'* ed. (a *1602*)
47 *iners cadat* ed. (*mers cadae 1602*)
48 *the . . . part* the breaking-off of my role

31–3 Hieronimo speaks first to the viceroy and then ('your daughter')
    to Castile. The son (l.33) is Lorenzo.
47 'Now let my hand fall idle'.

Printed by photolitho-offset
in Great Britain by
The Garden City Press Limited
Letchworth, Hertfordshire